OKLAHOMA

A Land and Its People:

Early Views and History in Picture Postcards

Dated December, 1920, this card gives an Easterner's view of early Oklahoma. It bears repeating:

"Having a fine time out with the Indians and halfbreeds. See nothing but oil and gas derricks—thousands of them. . . ."

Oklahoma, the last of continental America's lands of opportunity, is here reduced to an all too-well-known stereotype. Interestingly, what had formerly been seen as cause for embarrassment by some is now regarded with pride by all.

89ers Parade on Oklahoma Ave., Guthrie, Okla.

They came on horseback, they came by train, they came by wagon; some were even said to be pedalling bicycles or dashing across the line on foot. The occasion was the opening of the Unassigned Lands on April 22, 1889. We can imagine what it might have been like:

The crowd poised along the temporary borders was a half-wild bunch. Neither the admonitions of cavalry troops who had been sent to quell disturbances and to prevent any "Sooner" activity, nor the equally determined U.S. marshals and their assistants, could hold in check the enthusiasm and the tension of the crowds.

Meanwhile, the Indians looked on with wonder and resentment, and waited in silent resignation.

OKLAHOMA

A Land and Its People:

Early Views and History in Picture Postcards

by
Jack H. Smith

The Vestal Press Ltd.
Vestal, New York 13851

Dedication

for
my mother
Kathryn Smith
a woman devoted to her faith
and to the land she worked and loved

Acknowledgements

It is my pleasure to acknowledge the debt I owe to those whose assistance, patience, and encouragement made it possible for me to prepare this book. Mrs. Kathryn Stansbury has not only loaned postcards from her collection, but furnished me with invaluable insights and information. She is the sort of friend and advisor who makes the difficult less so, and offers encouragement when it is most needed. Thanks also to Mrs. C. S. Catlin from whom I purchased a few postcards.

This book could not have been completed without the proofreading and typing that my wife, Sherry, generously volunteered to do. In the last instance, although I hope He always remains foremost in all my endeavors, I wish to humbly acknowledge my appreciation to the God of all.

Jack H. Smith

Library of Congress Cataloging-in-Publication Data

Smith, Jack H.
  Oklahoma, a land and its people.

  Includes index.
  1. Oklahoma—Description and travel—Views.
2. Oklahoma—History, Local—Pictorial works.
3. Postcards—Oklahoma. I. Title.
F695.S63   1989   976.6   89-5642
ISBN 0-911572-80-5 (pbk.)

Introduction

With a history as rich and colorful as Oklahoma's, natives have every reason to exhibit pride. That history, like the land from which it springs and the people it involves, is incredibly diverse.

Oklahoma's history is the story of hard times, of good times, of success and failure. The frontier perserverance sustained our ancestors through drought, crop failure, inflationary cycles, economic depressions. Our history has been so rich, so diverse, so filled with such a marvelous and sometimes outrageous cast of characters that every Oklahoman should consider it his duty to learn as much about his home state and people as he possibly can—about the Sooners who crossed the starting lines too soon, about people like "Alfalfa" Murray, Jim Thorpe, Robert S. Kerr, and a host of others.

One of the reasons I began this book was to add what little I could to understanding the cultural, historical mosaic we call Oklahoma. Picture postcards have been chosen as the tools to examine the towns and people because first of all, picture postcards are history. They are first-hand pictorial accounts of the past. Even humorous cards furnish us with a look at the sorts of ideas that our parents and grandparents thought were funny. They are truthful representations of those days because they are from those days.

Early picture view cards of the type presented here can induce waves of nostalgia in the viewer—they reflect our childhoods and also the lives, habits, and surroundings of those who preceded us. The cards were sent through the mail; once received and read, they were often retained as keepsakes.

Sooners of every kind will recognize scenes from the past in these pages. Inside are pictures of street scenes, public buildings, hotels, private businesses, events, and people. The list of communities shown is large and covers every section of the state.

I hope that readers and viewers of this book will learn about Oklahoma communities other than their own and use the historical views to help them appreciate and understand a little better the Oklahoma of the past.

Jack H. Smith
December, 1988

Author's mother, far left, with four of her sisters, ca. 1940.

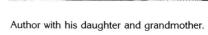

Author with his daughter and grandmother.

Editor's Preface

A number of very nice people from Oklahoma have been kind enough to help us out when we have needed to check information, and it is our pleasure to acknowledge their assistance: Frankie Herzer of the Plains Indians and Pioneers Museum; James W. Hubbard of Sapulpa; Karen Kirkpatrick of the Public Relations office, Phillips University; Marguerite Stokes of the Canadian County Historical Museum; Robert Powers of the Tulsa County Historical Society Museum; Wanda Green of the Pawnee Bill Museum; Barbara Kepper of the Tulsa Park and Recreation Department; Stella Campbell Rockwell of Enid; Judy McHenry of the University Relations office, The University of Tulsa; Kathy Jackson of the Public Information office, Oklahoma State University; Gabe Paxton of Choctaw Nation Indian Hospital in Talihina; and Ginger Larew of the Oklahoma State Historical Society.

We are always interested in improving our publications. Your suggestions and comments are most welcome; please feel free to bring to our attention any information which would be of value in future printings.

Grace L. Houghton
The Vestal Press, Ltd.
PO Box 97
Vestal, NY 13851-0097

123056

Ada is one of many Oklahoma towns with a colorful history. Near the present site of the town is the birthplace of the only Oklahoma governor born in what was, at that time, Indian Territory. He was Oklahoma's twelfth chief executive: Robert S. Kerr.

Perhaps the single most memorable event in the town's past revolves around assassin Jim Miller. Miller was reported to have killed over two dozen men, including the legendary Pat Garrett in New Mexico, but his murder of respected Ada townsman Gus Bobbitt was more than the local residents could endure. A group of them took Miller from the jail one night and lynched him.

The first building in the area of Ada served both as a store and residence of Jeff Reed who named the fledgling community in honor of his daughter. Erection of a post office in the following year (1890) marked the town's founding. Ada is the home of East Central University, which opened in 1909. Land around the town is noted for its livestock and crops (cotton, wheat, corn, and hay). Ada's growth has also been due to manufacturing (flour milling, glass, furniture, and cement making).

Northwestern State Normal School, Alva, Okla.

Located in the Cherokee Outlet not far from the Kansas border, Alva was selected in 1893 as one of the land office towns at the opening of the Outlet. Alva Adams, an attorney for the Sante Fe Railroad—which had made the site one of its stops—gave the community its name. Small as it was, Alva became the setting for Northwestern State College, the second oldest (1897) normal—or teachers'—college in the state. The Cherokee Outlet Museum in Alva provides excellent examples of Oklahoma history preservation.

WICHITA GRASS HOUSE. ANADARKO, OKLA.

These round grass houses are examples of structures constructed by the Wichita Indians during the 17th through the 19th centuries—not all Indians lived in tepees (or tipis). The Wichita Indians considered the areas of modern Texas, Oklahoma, and Arkansas to be their territory. As did many other Indian tribes who learned to coexist with the elements, they were part-time hunters and part-time farmers, taking only what nature offered without disrupting the natural balance and cycles of plant and animal.

Main Street looking West, Anadarko, Okla.

Well known today for its Indian institutions and background, Anadarko was a town with broad streets and slow-paced living in the beginning of this century. Founded in 1901 during the last of the land runs, Anadarko's Main Street is shown here as it was in about 1910. Formerly the home of the Southern Plains Indian Agency which served tribes in Oklahoma, Kansas and Texas, Anadarko's Federal Building was decorated by members of the Kiowa tribe.

The current museums and places of interest have a decided Indian flavor. They include the Anadarko Philomathic Museum, the Southern Plains Indian Museum and Crafts Center, Fort Cobb State Park, and the National Hall of Fame for famous American Indians. The most frequently visited area is Indian City, located a few miles outside of town, where village reconstructions of several Plains and Southwest Indian tribes are featured. Tepees, tools, and cooking utensils give authenticity to the site. The atmosphere of Indian City suggests the simplicity of early life in the territory.

Much of Oklahoma is cotton-growing country. For farmers who planted it, cotton was a crop that greatly contributed to the household budget. Cattle, hay, corn, and (later) soybeans rounded out the list of crops that could be raised. The typical small farm, especially before 1940, could not justify sinking family funds into purchasing machinery for picking cotton; generally it was picked by hand.

Ardmore was founded on the site of the Roff Brothers' "700 Ranch," where the Atchison, Topeka and Santa Fe Railroad laid track in 1887. Ardmore prospered slowly, but continuously.

During the first few decades of the 20th century, cotton, cattle, and oil were very important to Ardmore's economy.

This post card showing wagons loaded with bales of cotton was postmarked in 1913, the year oil was discovered in the area of Ardmore.

Senior High School, Ardmore, Okla.—2

Though at first the search for oil near Ardmore lacked promise, Roy Johnson raised every penny for drilling that he could by selling property and borrowing money—even from his fiancée—to finance the venture. Oil did appear eventually and Johnson, the newspaperman, became Johnson, the oil baron.

John Ringling, one of the Ringling Circus brothers, was also a local petroleum prospector whose wells were several miles outside of Ardmore. To expedite the delivery of his liquid gold into town, Ringling paid for laying railroad track from his wells to Ardmore, aiding the community and the railroad at the same time.

MAIN STREET, ARDMORE, OKLAHOMA

As one of the few Oklahoma towns dating before the 1889 land run, Ardmore assumed a position of some prestige. This view shows a clean, commercially active downtown area stretching beyond the horizon.

In recent years Ardmore's reputation as a recreation center has been enhanced by the popularity of nearby Arbuckle Mountains and Lake Murray State Park. In the town itself are the Charles Goddard Center with its collection of Western art, and the Eliza Cruce Hall Doll Collection which has received international recognition.

4

The Main Thoroughfare of Atoka, Oklahoma

Atoka, named after a Choctaw chief, was established in 1867 by a Baptist missionary, Reverend J. S. Murrow. He also founded the Atoka Baptist Academy.

For many Oklahomans who lived in the central and eastern parts of the state, an automobile trip to Dallas—often taken to view the annual college football classic between the Universities of Oklahoma and Texas—meant a brief, but pleasant drive through Atoka.

Essentially Oklahoman in character and flavor, Atoka's residents were friendly, if a bit taciturn until they got to know you, which is to say in their own words, "until they got the measure of what you were about."

Even with that caution, Atoka was a busy place. Note the cars parked in front of the local business establishments—from Oklahoma's Public Service Company to the hardware and five-and-dime stores that have now all but disappeared from the Southwest. The Main Street Cafe seen here was another typical, welcome sight in much of small-town America.

Carnegie Library, Bartlesville, Okla.

Andrew Carnegie, whether through public spiritedness, Christian charity, or as a lasting testament to himself, spent the first few decades of the twentieth century sponsoring public library buildings in selected cities and towns throughout the United States. Several were built in Oklahoma, including this one in Bartlesville.

Maire Hotel, Bartlesville, Okla.—22

As a city which flexed its economic muscle early on, Bartlesville quickly became a beacon for salesmen, entrepreneurs, and young men attracted to the glamour of the petroleum industry and opportunities to start a career or to begin afresh. The Maire Hotel was a Bartlesville landmark that saw them come and go, or come and stay. Thoughtful service and filling meals, especially the noteworthy breakfasts, enhanced the hotel's oustanding reputation.

First M. E. Church, Bartlesville, Okla.

Methodism was established in Oklahoma during the state's formative years, and in some Oklahoma towns one of the largest places of worship is the local Methodist Church. Bartlesville's First M. E. Church is an impressive building which serves as a stately monument to the importance of religion to early citizens.

Y. M. C. A., Bartlesville, Okla.

Founded in the late 1870's when trader Jake Bartles built the first flour mill in Indian Territory, Bartlesville's history has been robust, beginning with a simple trading business among local Indians and proceeding through the discovery of oil to the establishment of various industries. The town has become a mecca in northeastern Oklahoma. The Y.M.C.A. building is particularly impressive when one considers that the population did not exceed 15,000 in the 1920's.

Catholic Church, Bartlesville, Okla.—16

Since its early days, Oklahoma has maintained a strong Protestant tradition, so producers of picture postcards supplied their "Sooner" customers with views of a landscape dotted with Baptist, Methodist, Presbyterian, and (later) Pentecostal and Evangelical churches. Catholics met a lot of prejudice, but established footholds and built churches such as this one Bartlesville. This view was produced by E. C. Kropp of Milwaukee, a postcard publisher who photographed and printed view cards from locations all over the United States.

Phillip Bldg. and First National Bank Bldg., Bartlesville, Okla.—18

The oblong structure in front, housing the First National Bank, was built first. The addition of the Phillips Building at its rear created the sort of imposing view one would normally expect in cities much larger in size and population than Bartlesville.

Woolaroc Museum outside of Bartlesville housing paintings by Frederic Remington and Charles Marion Russell, and its wildlife preserve are only two examples of the generosity of Frank Phillips, founder of Phillips Petroleum. His $50,000 donation to build the Bartlesville Senior High School-Junior College and his multiple gifts of money to the University of Oklahoma and other historical/cultural institutions make it easy to understand how Phillips became the only non-Indian to be made a member of the Osage tribe, the group to whom he dedicated the Woolaroc Museum.

Frank Phillip's Residence, Bartlesville, Okla.

Bartlesville has maintained a dominant presence in Oklahoma due in part to the philanthropy and drive of oilman Frank Phillips. The house pictured here, completed by 1910, features Ionic columns, verandas, second-level porches, and a striking barn-red roof. The interior boasted marble, exotic woods from all over the world, famous paintings, and oriental rugs. Generous when it came to making contributions and dedicated to making both his adopted city and state better for his presence, Phillips clearly also lived well himself.

Bartlesville Zinc Co., Bartlesville, Okla.—14

Bartlesville's economy was not totally dependent on petrolem; zinc smelting began in 1906. In today's city the attractions include the Tom Mix museum, Phillips' exhibit hall, the Frank Phillips mansion, and a replica of Oklahoma's first commercial oil well known as the Nellie Johnstone.

Federal Bldg., Blackwell, Okla.—4

Many Oklahoma towns have a colorful, romantic background and Blackwell is no exception. Although the town's founding dates to 1893, its history is of even earlier vintage. People determined to settle in the Unassigned Lands with or without help from the government were called "Boomers". In the 1880's such a group led by adventurer and self-promoter David L. Payne crossed into the area of present-day Blackwell, built temporary living accommodations, and planted crops. Payne and his company were removed from the location— just as they had been on three earlier attempts at settlement in the territory.

It was, in part, the agitation of these Boomers as well as a growing feeling that the territory should be opened up for settlement that led to the Great Land Run of 1889 and then to subsequent runs, culminating in the final runs of 1901 and 1906.

Junior High School, Blackwell, Oklahoma

The official founding of Blackwell was September, 1893, when the Cherokee Outlet of which it was a part was opened for settlement by a "run." The founder, A. J. Blackwell, claimed ownership due to his status as an adopted citizen of the Cherokee Nation. He established the first town government and placed himself at its head.

Blackwell's rule was as autocratic as those of the political machines in Cincinnati and Chicago, and of New York City's Tammany Hall. Blackwell also created a role for himself as a self-ordained Baptist minister, a title which did not seem appropriate for a man who had two accusations of murder levelled against him. Again, as did Cincinnati, Chicago, and New York City, the town of Blackwell survived the political corruption and even prospered.

(AAA)   GIBSON'S MODERN CAMP AND APARTMENTS, CHANDLER, OKLA.   (AAA)

Chandler, a community very near the center of Oklahoma, is similar in some respects to other Oklahoma towns. It was founded almost midway between Oklahoma City and Tulsa in 1891 and named for President Benjamin Harrison's Assistant Secretary of the Interior. Many of the state's other cities were also named either for people with a connection to Oklahoma's formative years or for someone of national prominence.

Chandler has suffered devastation from that most feared of Oklahoma's natural enemies—the tornado. A twister that touched down and stayed down for too long in 1897 killed 14 people and destroyed every building in the town except the local Presbyterian Church where a group of citizens had sought refuge. Chandler's connection with organized religion continues; the Church of God has rented the large picnic area outside of town for several years as the site of their State Camp Meeting.

10

5 North School, Chickasha, Okla.

This brick structure which features contrasting stone is North School in Chickasha, built at the turn of the century. The author attended this grammar school in the early 1950's and can remember the awe which the building inspired. Erected at the turn of the century, it was still a solid edifice when the author won there a "Certificate of Merit" in a tug-of-war in May, 1953. The grounds behind the building were used for running races and other track and field activities.

This picture was taken in 1910. Close examination of the students standing in the front school yard reveals that they are wearing the obligatory soft cloth cap and, except for one boy in a white shirt, the often oversized, wide-lapel coat.

City Hall and Fire Department, Chickasha, Okla.—1

The southwestern Oklahoma city of Chickasha, founded in 1892, was chosen for a station stop and division point on the Rock Island Railroad. Before that, the area was along the famous Chisholm Trail, which extended from Texas to Kansas and along which millions of cattle were driven.

Chickasha was never a boom town, but during its early years, it grew like one. Originally granted to the Choctaws, the entire territory was assigned in the 1830's to the Chickasaws, from whom town took its name.

The practical citizens of the community saw fit to combine their city hall and fire departments into one building.

11

Residences of — D. H. Signon Residence. — Chickasha, Okla.

Ben Hampton Residence.

H. B. Johnson Residence.

Like towns the world over, Chickasha had some well-to-do citizens. The owners of these residences, D. H. Signon, Ben Hampton, and H. B. Johnson were men known by most, if not all, of the city's inhabitants in the early twentieth century.

The man who mailed this card in 1911 does not focus on the homes shown here, but apparently on the opportunity for work. It reads:

Dear Earl,
Received your card today and I want you to come to Chickasha. I am working on the girl's industrial school and I am boarding at 1600 West Minnesota. Take Dakota car to the boarding house. Get off at 16th street, walk a block north and a block west or come out to the school building. If in the daytime, take any car. Jim.

Chickasha was a working man's town. Both Harold Sapp, a Scot short of stature but long on work habits who painted many of the community's buildings, and a rangy young fellow named Kenneth Smith of Irish and Indian ancestry who drove a local cab and performed the duties of a nightclub bouncer and occasional tinsmith, called Chickasha their home. The author knew them both—one as parent, the other as maternal grandfather. They, like so many of Chickasha's citizens, were simple people of few pretensions but multiple abilities.

Fine Arts Building, O.C.W. Chickasha, Okla.

The Oklahoma College for Women (now the University of Sciences and Arts of Oklahoma) was an institution of which Chickasha was justifiably proud. Founded in 1908 by the newly formed state legislature, seventeed buildings were built on the seventy-five acre grounds.

The Fine Arts Building shown here gives an idea of the modern architectural style employed in its planning. At the time of its erection, O. C. W. was one of the few state-supported women's colleges in the United States. A swimming pool in the Physical Education Hall, fields for outdoor sporting events, six tennis courts, and even a couple of golf putting greens were among its features. A 140-acre farm attached to the college served as an experimental station and was maintained by the Department of Biology.

Visitors to Chickasha have remarked on the friendliness of the town. Part of the reason for this, of course, has to do with Southern hospitality; Oklahomans have always identified themselves with both the American South and West.

Shannoan Springs Park—with a picturesque lake and the city zoo—was indicative of the city's commitment to culture and recreation. At this particular park, as the author recalls, were held public festivals, Easter egg hunts with prizes, musical extravaganzas, and a buffalo barbeque on at least one occasion.

Established by the state legislature in 1920, the Oklahoma Military Academy was built near Claremore on grounds adjacent to today's Will Rogers Memorial.

Although not as remote as this picture suggests, the proximity to civilization did not distract the young cadets from acquiring their education. The strict regimen of "The West Point of the Southwest" insured that those sent here kept their attention and energies focused on the academy itself.

Along with the necessary appointment, graduation from O. M. A. entitled the student/soldier to admittance to the Army's West Point Military Academy without the otherwise mandatory entrance examination. Misbehaving students in Oklahoma's high schools were sometimes promised enrollment at the academy unless conduct improved. The threats were probably ineffective, but the institution certainly instilled a high regard for its disciplinary standards.

"I never met a man I didn't like" reads the message at the base of this bronze statue, which was completed in 1938 by sculptor Jo Davidson in time for the Will Rogers Memorial Museum opening. A duplicate is located in the nation's capital. Rogers began a relationship without any prejudice or ill will. He honestly looked for—and expected—the best from everyone he encountered. He must have been disappointed on a regular basis, but he did a good job of camouflaging it. The museum in which this statue is housed was built of stone quarried locally.

"I never met a man I didst like"

WILL ROGERS
1879—1935

In the New Will Rogers Memorial Building, Claremore, Oklahoma

Located on the grounds of the Will Rogers Memorial is this bronze tribute to the humorist which shows Rogers as a humble cowboy. Years of association with Flo Ziegfeld of Follies fame, familiarity with Hollywood, the popularity of his radio programs and newspaper columns, and even visits to the White House did not alter Rogers' down-to-earth nature. He was a man who loved a good joke, a bowl of chili, and a new lariat trick. This piece of sculpture was financed by private funds.

ONC.81—"Riding into the Sunset," Will Rogers Monument, Claremore, Oklahoma

14

The Oklahoma community of Coalgate, as its name suggests, was closely linked with coal mining. In fact, Coalgate was a center for this industry and a chief supplier of coal to surrounding towns at a time when coal was important for both heating and cooking. The oil and gas industries with which Oklahoma is so closely connected soon overshadowed the coal industry; the town's growth, like that of other Oklahoma communities that produced tons of the black rock, stabilized for a while at pre-1920 numbers and then declined.

Lee School Building, erected at the turn of the century, was an early monument to local education.

The story of Dewey's founding is told often, but still remains interesting. It seems that J. H. Bartles, the man who founded Bartlesville, was an entrepreneur of the first order. When he considered the profits that his store could make closer to a railroad stop, Bartles moved the store on rollers to a new location a few miles away. This 1898 feat is particularly impressive because Bartles kept the store open for business during the five months it took to make the move.

The town was named for Admiral Dewey, whose recent naval victory at Manila Bay against the Spanish made him a national hero. Of more than local interest is the Tom Mix Museum, built to honor the rodeo and cowboy movie star whose career included a short-lived stint in Dewey as a lawman.

Another area through which the Chisholm Trail ran was Duncan, originally named for trader William Duncan. The former tailor had the good fortune to marry a Chickasaw who converted her Indian land allotment into a sizable fortune. She demanded that her five hundred acres be the same land through which the Rock Island Railway would run and upon which the town would be built. She then sold lots to businessmen, pioneers, and speculators who recognized the value of the holdings.

The Duncan area was included in one of the last land openings in 1901. The Halliburton Oil Well Cementing Company, founded in Duncan, has become an international firm with revenues among the largest of any Oklahoma company. The Stephens County Historical Museum's Indian and pioneer exhibits, which include an old school house, warrant a place on every tourist's itinerary.

Science Hall, S. T. C. College, Durant, Okla.

Durant, Oklahoma, became familiar to many Oklahomans as a town they passed through on Highway 69 South on the way to Dallas, Texas. Anyone who has ever made the trip and taken time to explore the town has been pleasantly surprised. Durant is the home of Southeastern Oklahoma State University, formerly Southeastern State College, founded in 1901. The community is surrounded by grazing grasslands and fertile farmlands. Choctaw Indian Dixon Durant owned the ranch land upon which the city began.

16

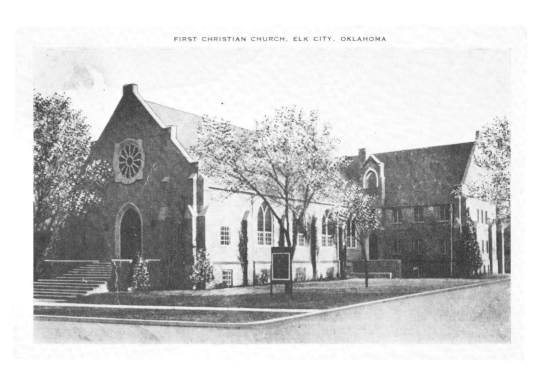

FIRST CHRISTIAN CHURCH, ELK CITY, OKLAHOMA

At first, Elk City was the rest stop on major cattle drives from Texas to Kansas. One story states that the community adopted the name "Busch" with some measure of anticipation that a brewery would locate there. Some of the more sober-minded citizens, incensed that their town would carry the same name as a beer label, made their protests heard. Another story says the town was renamed because "Bausch" was the name given to another Oklahoma post office. Whatever the case, the town decided to call itself "Elk City" after Indian Chief Elk River, also the man for whom Elk Creek outside of town was named. This western Oklahoma community is famous for the Rodeo of Champions staged annually on Labor Day.

Elk City's fortunes were connected to the discovery of oil in the region during the 1940's.

High School, El Reno, Okla.

Initially named Reno City, this western Oklahoma community changed its handle—and its location—when the Rock Island Railroad laid its track on the other side of the river. The adaptable and enterprising citizens promptly moved the entire town—buildings and all—to the railroad's location.

The town's name was related to Fort Reno, named after Civil War General Jesse L. Reno. For a brief period, Fort Reno was the residence of western artist Frederic Remington (1861-1909).

El Reno became a center for flour milling and transportation. After the Rock Island Railroad finally made El Reno an important point for conducting its business, railroad cars being loaded and unloaded became a familiar sight.

Tourist attractions include the Canadian County Historical Society Museum and the remains of Fort Reno.

17

MOTEL CONWAY
EL RENO, OKLAHOMA

The sight of these roadside motels is a familiar one seen on both coasts and everywhere in between. El Reno, situated along Interstate 40 (formerly Route 66), is a well-known stopping place for motorists travelling either east or west. Far enough from Oklahoma City proper to allow more modest rates at its motels, it's a large enough town to provide everything that a traveller might need.

During the 1940's, western curio shops that stocked Indian dolls, state insignias on everything from tee-shirts to ashtrays, and miscellaneous became frequent sights along major highways.

Springs Park, Enid, Okla.

Formerly known as Government Springs Park, this area in Enid was a watering place on the Chisholm Trail, and the Cherokee Indians used to camp here before the land run. The springs also provided a source of water for crews constructing the railroad. Through the twenties and thirties this pretty park was a center for family picnics, and the Enid High School May Queen was crowned on this bridge as part of the annual celebration. As the town grew larger and expanded farther north and west, other parks were established and this park was no longer kept up as well, and most of the springs were capped.

18

High School, Enid, Okla.—16

Since opening in 1912, Enid High School has been greatly enlarged, but the original section is still in use. Through the years the school has maintained a band, an orchestra, and a sports program of which townspeople are proud.

Convention Hall, Enid. Okla.—13

Like the high school, the Convention Center has been expanded and the original part is still in use. Another big building on the south side of the city square is connected to the old building which has both ground-level seating and balcony seating. The complex is now known as the Cherokee Strip Conference Center.

Located in north central Oklahoma in an area previously known as the Cherokee Outlet, the city began when that section was opened for settlement in September, 1893. Actually, Enid had been populated before that date. A year earlier, the United States selected the site as a government land office in the outlet and sent surveyors with a detachment of cavalry troops to prepare for the run and set the town's perimeters.

19

Grand Avenue. ENID, Okla.

One of the stories about how Enid received its name tells of cattle drivers on the Chisholm Trail who, like the later government surveyors, stopped at the site which became Springs Park. A few of the more adventuresome cowboys turned the "Dine" sign on the cook's tent upside down, thus creating the name "Enid."

The trolley wire and track show that this progressive city was taking advantage of the high-tech transportation of the day. Streetcars ran out to the university and past the high school.

Bird's-Eye View of Enid, Okla.

Enid's history includes some turbulent times. One story tells about a group of Cherokee Indians who wanted to profit from town growth by acquiring allotments in the proposed townsite. The furor caused by this reached such proportions that then Secretary of the Interior, Hoke Smith, ordered the town separated into North Enid and South Enid. He also ordered that an area three miles to the south of the original site be the true town center.

The Rock Island Railway maintained its ticket office in North Enid, refusing to be moved. Eventually, tempers cooled but not before a Rock Island train was sabotaged by weakened bridge supports near South Enid. A presidential proclamation issued in September, 1894, enforced Hoke Smith's ruling, but the bitterness between the two factions was not soon forgotten.

This view of Enid looks over the square downtown; Broadway now cuts across the square.

The Enid of the 1890's is removed from the Enid of the late nineteenth and early twentieth centuries. The earlier settlement had to contend with crop failures while religious activities shared the spotlight with gambling houses and saloons. Enid's background paralleled that of many other Oklahoma communities where men afraid of neither work nor fighting, and women who cooked, raised children, and shared in the hard manual labor of their husbands' daily struggle. It was hard for a person not toughened to life on the prairie or in the forests to survive those first Oklahoma years. With medical advancement, survival became easier. The Enid General Hospital and Clinic provided a landmark in Enid's medical history; now Enid has several hospitals.

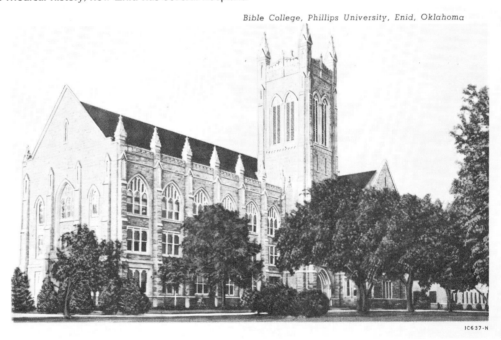

Bible College, Phillips University, Enid, Oklahoma

Established in 1906 as Oklahoma Christian University, this institution was renamed in 1912 in honor of the school's chief benefactor, T. W. Phillips of New Castle, Pennsylvania. The college was originally located on a farm on the east edge of town and until recently the whole institution was run by the Disciples of Christ. The Bible College enrollment has typically been constituted almost half of the student body. In 1988 the city of Enid bought the buildings of the non- Bible School division, and now leases them back to the school. Proceeds from this arrangement go to scholarships for students in the Enid area. The two divisions are now completely autonomous.

A co-educational institution, Phillips boasts a prestigious music department, an important Indian collection, and an impressive list of botanical specimens. The Marshall Building pictured here is one of the early buildings and is known as the seminary building which houses the Phillips Graduate Seminary.

Enid's current list of attractions includes The Museum of the Cherokee Strip which opened in 1975, the Mid-America Summerfest, and the Grand National Quail Hunt held each December.

Western Oklahoma territory had been ceded to non-indigenous Indian tribes to punish the Five Civilized Tribes and other Oklahoma Indians who had rebelled against the United States during the Civil War. The Plains Indians who had previously occupied the entire western portion of the state were not pleased with this arrangement. Because of their frequent attacks against white settlers living in the region, Fort Sill, near Lawton, was built in 1869 as a prairie outpost.

Old Guard House, Fort Sill, Okla.

Few frontier army posts have been the residence of more illustrious men of American history than Fort Sill, Oklahoma— from Quanah Parker to Geronimo to the unsuccessful haberdasher and later President of the United States, Harry S. Truman (Truman was stationed at Camp Doniphan). Now a museum, the old guard house once served as the prison for Geronimo.

Old Stockade, Fort Sill, Okla.

One of the most famous Fort Sill residents was the tactically brilliant Comanche War Chief, Quanah Parker. Against overwhelming odds and superior weaponry, Parker led his braves on daring, successful raids. In his efforts to maintain territory for the Comanches and knowing that a war of attrition is won by the side with greater numbers, Parker laid down his weapons to save his people from needless sacrifice, even though his reputation for winning was still intact.

Parker then devoted his life to helping his people adapt. Through his negotiations and statesman-like conduct, Parker enriched the Comanche people both financially and socially. Parker, who had seven wives and twenty-four children, attained local and national distinction. He was president of the local school board, official Comanche representative to Washington, held stock in the Quanah, Acme and Pacific Railway, and even found time to be a farmer and a rancher. Parker lies buried by his mother; the gravesite is marked with an eighteen-foot red granite monument.

Officers Quarters, Ft. Sill, Lawton, Okla.

Warfare in Europe in 1917-18 made it amply clear that the horse cavalry was an outmoded form of military activity, but traditions die hard in the military establishment and horses continued to serve in the army until the middle 1930's.

Although motorized transport was in use at Fort Sill as elsewhere by 1914, the base continued to use the horse as in earlier days. Fort Sill in the 1800's was a cavalry camp, but in later years has served the nation as an artillery base.

A favorite soldiers' activity is "going to the show." For recruits and seasoned soldiers alike, the movies give an opportunity to escape the barracks.

Fort Sill, especially with the Wichita Mountains in the distant background forming a shapely horizon to orange and gold sunsets, is considered by many to be a beautiful place. But for those accustomed to the lifestyles of cities like Chicago, New York, or Los Angeles, the show house can be a welcomed diversion from military duties at a base likely to be thought by them as windswept and dull.

Historic Chapel, Old Post, Fort Sill, Okla.

9A887-N

Geronimo was one of Fort Still's most famous residents, noted for having withstood up to five thousand whites with his band of thirty-eight Chiricahua Apaches. Brought to Fort Sill in 1894, the aged warrior insisted on making his own living rather than allowing himself to become dependent on those who were once his enemies. After a brief period of incarceration at Fort Sill, Geronimo was allowed a large measure of freedom. He took part in rodeos, world's fairs, and parades; he even met Theodore Roosevelt and no doubt considered that Roosevelt had the greater honor. He sold his own hand-made bows and arrows and hawked pictures of himself to tourists. Geronimo died in 1909, but the government did not permit his remains to be returned to his Arizona home territory even for burial.

The old chapel seen here was built in 1875 and has served as both a church and a school. Services are conducted here today, and the building is open to tourists.

POST OFFICE, FREDERICK, OKLAHOMA

Since early times, cotton and wheat were Frederick's principal crops, although cotton was the mainstay as evidenced by the cotton mills and compresses in the town. The Cotton Carnival, an annual November event, is celebrated in Frederick, which has been described as one of the cleanest and friendliest towns in Oklahoma or the U.S.

In the 1940's, two cotton compresses and a cottonseed oil mill operated most of the year, proof of the importance of the white crop to this small Oklahoma town. Frederick was the recipient of a Carnegie Library building and is home to a College of Business.

In the Cotton Yard, Frederick, Okla.

First State House, Guthrie, Okla.

The tent city which Guthrie became on its first day of settlement in April, 1889, was soon replaced by more substantial buildings. By the end of its first week of existence, the town boasted frame stores, land offices, and lawyer's quarters—all open for brisk and steady business—the result of hard work and pre-cut, numbered lumber.

The prairie was transformed into a thriving city which served as the Oklahoma territorial capital from 1907 to 1910. The first state house, seen here, later became the Logan County Court House.

OKLAHOMA AVENUE, LOOKING EAST, GUTHRIE, OKLA.

Although the population of Guthrie never exceeded several thousand, ambitious undertakings became successful completions. The world's largest Scottish Rite Masonic Temple, even more inspiring on the inside than on the outside, is located here as is the Pollard Theatre where famous talent has performed, the first Oklahoma State House, the State Capital Publishing Museum, and the Oklahoma Territorial Museum.

26

Oklahoma Bldg. Guthrie, Okla.

The Great Land Run of 1889 was the first page in modern Oklahoma history. That page, however, is not written clearly. In the agitation to open the territory for white settlement prior to the Run, Boomer leader David L. Payne (a cousin of Davy Crockett) is often seen as a leading figure. His court battles and forceful personality are given credit for setting the stage for the Run, although Payne's role in the whole affair is occasionally exaggerated.

Contributions of other men are often overlooked. Judge Theodore Sears from Ottawa, Kansas, was a counsel for the Missouri, Kansas and Texas (KATY) Railroad. As early as 1879 he advocated opening the Unassigned Lands. His descriptions of rich, fertile land were intended to encourage prospective homesteaders, at the same time he was suggesting that the government had best open up before "The people. . .take the matter into their own hands."

Congressmen Springer, Van Wyck, Weaver, and Clarke prepared bills for the opening of the land for settlement which failed to pass. Undaunted, they re-introduced the measure to Congress in 1886 with the additional signature of Missouri's representative, Charles Mansur. Finally in 1889 the bill was attached to the Indian Appropriations Act which forced its signing by President Grover Cleveland on March 3, 1889. With this piece of legislation, Guthrie became part of the first great land rush in Oklahoma history. Oklahoma itself, as a separate entity, was a year away from existence.

St. Joseph Retreat, Guthrie, Okla.

Guthrie became one of the centers of Catholic education in Oklahoma, and in 1916 Benedictine nuns received a charter to operate a four-year liberal arts school. Originally, the institution was known as St. Joseph's Academy; later it became Oklahoma Catholic College for Women. In 1919 the Oklahoma legislature authorized the school to grant college degrees.

Packing Elberta Peaches. **Guthrie, Okla.**

Made in Germany.   F. B. Lillie & Co., Importers & Publishers, Guthrie, Okla.

Peach trees as well as pecan trees, apple trees, and even an occasional orange or lemon tree grow in Oklahoma's nutrient-rich soils. When the fruit is ripe for picking, work proceeds at a furious pace to load bushels into waiting trucks to rush the product to market; the liesurely pose shown in this postcard is deceptive.

Modern-day tourists visiting Guthrie can have a special treat by partaking of these fine fruits of the land.

PIONEER DAY GUYMON OKLA — 1937

Guymon is the largest community in the Oklahoma panhandle. In 1971, the American Cattleman's Association announced the relocation of the fat cattle and slaughtering capital of the United States to Guymon, a boon for the town of eight thousand people.

It doesn't take an old-timer to realize that Oklahoma is a state that loves its celebrations and festivals. Pioneer Day in Guymon commemorates the addition of the panhandle to Oklahoma through passage of the Organic Act of 1890. Oklahomans are joined by Texans and Kansans for activities that include free barbecued buffalo, high- stepping parades, and a local rodeo that attracts talented performers from all over the United States.

These real-photo postcards date to the mid-thirties. Barely discernible on this card are twins dressed as cowboys who are being pushed in a buggy. Fedoras and caps are scattered in a sea of Stetsons. Also in the parade is an Abraham Lincoln wearing a stovepipe hat, and a prairie wagon preceding a group of rodeo stars on horseback.

Named for Joe Heavener, local merchant and friend of the Indians in the area, the town of Heavener rests at the base of Poteau Mountain. Mr. Heavener owned the land upon which the community grew. The Choctaws of the region identified the area around Heavener as the "prairie of the tall grass."

Main Street, Hennessey, Okla.

Hennessey was one of the towns established during the Land Run of 1889. It took the name of freight hauler Patrick Hennessey, who was attacked by the Indians and killed while travelling through the area in 1874. Hennessey was on his way southward along the Chisholm Trail heading for Fort Sill with two wagonloads of oats when the ambush occurred.

This postcard shows the broad dirt road of Hennessey that was typical of Oklahoma's first Main Streets. Also typical were the buggies and wagons lined up in front of the frame and brick buildings.

Exceptional views like this give accurate detail of a time not so long ago.

U. S. Post Office, Henryetta, Okla.

Henryetta has been a major employer for citizens of surrounding communities since its beginning in 1900 when the St. Louis and San Francisco Railway Company (the Frisco) selected this site through which to lay track. Glass making, zinc smelting, and coal mining are the principal industries, along with raising livestock and farming the area's rich land. The surrounding pasture land has supported every imaginable type of livestock, including imported breeds. The fertile topsoil and sand combination is ideal for producing a variety of melons and other vegetables. Present-day Henryetta is proud of being the home of five-time world champion cowboy Jim Shoulders.

School Building, Hobart, Okla.

Hobart, the county seat of Kiowa County in southeastern Oklahoma, was opened for settlement in the 1901. Except for the area involving the town of Apache to the north of Lawton which was opened by a legitimate run, the 1901 land openings were characterized by lotteries and public auction of lots (as in the case of Lawton). Almost 170,000 people registered in the land offices at Fort Sill and El Reno for the 2,080,000 acres of land in what was to become Kiowa, Caddo, and Comanche counties. Between July 29 and August 5, 1901 13,000 names were drawn, each to receive one-hundred-and-sixty-acre plots.

Hobart is in an area that had formerly belonged to the Kiowa Indians. The region's rich farmlands produce cotton, hay, and sorghum and are also valuable for cattle grazing.

THERE'S FINE FISHING
AT IDABEL, OKLAHOMA

At the Oklahoma entrance to Ouachita National Forest, Idabel enjoys the serenity and natural beauty of the southeastern part of the state. Along with oak, maple, and dogwood trees are pine and other indigenous trees which add to the New England look of the area.

The romantic scene shown here was a popular invention of postcard manufacturers; but in this case, the setting, if not the message, has some truth attached to it.

Kingfisher, located on the Chisholm Trail, was part of the original Unassigned Lands opened for settlement in 1889. The church shown in the picture indicates an established religious community by the time the card was produced.

The town was named for rancher and stage-line operator King Fisher. Called "the buckle of the wheat belt," the town was also the location for Kingfisher College, founded in 1894; it operated independently for thirty-three years before becoming part of the University of Oklahoma.

Saint Paul's Catholic Church, Kingfisher, Okla.

City Hall, Lawton, Okla.

Founded six days after the Kiowa Comanche Reservation Lands were opened for settlement, Lawton's birth on August 6, 1901, was different from the settling of the reservation's remaining areas. Names were drawn for most of those areas, but the land around Lawton was sold at public auction. Successful bidders were required to deposit $25 as down payment and given thirty minutes to bring in the remainder, or the lot was resold. Prices for the lots ranged from a couple hundred dollars to $4,500 for one hotly contested town site.

Saloons and gambling houses that were rapidly established in the new town soon gave way to more respectable businesses.

Court House, Lawton, Okla.

Lawton was named for Army General Henry Lawton, a popular American hero. Lawton was noted for outstanding courage displayed in battles from the Civil War to the Spanish American War. He was killed by a sniper's bullet in the Philippines. Naming the town after a military figure was appropriate, given the proximity of Fort Sill.

This view of the original Lawton Court House shows a structure of impressive proportions, but the building soon proved to be too small to handle Comanche County's legal and federal affairs and it was replaced in 1939 by a three-story building of sandstone and steel.

Lawton High School Building, Lawton, Oklahoma.

It is no secret that some of Oklahoma's early history is filled with accounts of blood feuds, rowdyism, and generally uninspiring conduct. Lawton's first days witnessed the building of dozens of saloons and places of questionable social value.

The story of a sign which proclaimed "All Nations Welcome Here Except Carrie" (referring to the axe-swinging prohibitionist crusader from Kansas) indicates some pretty boisterous goings-on. Ultimately, however, a city should be judged on the basis of its contributions to the general culture. As related earlier, Lawton did rid itself of most of its unsavory characters and as the large high school on this 1908 postcard shows, the city was quick to put its money, energy, and talent into beautifying its surroundings and educating its youth.

33

Crucifixion Scene, Sunrise Easter Service in the Wichita Mountains, near Lawton, Okla.

In the 1930's, the W. P. A. (a Federal program during the Roosevelt administration in the 1930's that put unemployed citizens to work in construction; the initials stand for 'Works Progress Administration') built the Holy Land setting in the Wichita Mountains where the pageant is held. The actors, all volunteers, are dressed in period costumes that, with a stage setting of the ancient city of Jerusalem, leaves an impression that is not soon forgotten. Perhaps the greatest accolade is the comparison made between these performances and the German Passion Play at Oberammergau.

Thousands attend Lawton's Easter Sunrise Service which includes the triumphal entry and crucifixion.

Many places in America stage religious plays at both outdoor and indoor theaters, but few of them have been in existence longer than this one. Lawton's pageant began in 1925. The setting is ideal because the Wichita Mountains are reminiscent of Holy Land terrain. More than fifty scenes from the Life of Christ begin with His birth and proceed through His ministry, crucifixion, and resurrection.

Triumphal Entry, Easter Sunrise Service, in the Wichita Mountains, near Lawton, Okla.

The Chapel, Sunrise Easter Service in the Wichita Mountains, near Lawton, Okla.

In 1975, a twenty-four-foot tall representation of Christ was erected in the Wichita Mountains as a beacon. The statue weighs eight thousand pounds and is of white marble. This representation was part of the vision of The Reverend Mark Wallock, founder of the Easter Sunrise Service.

This 1910 postcard produced for the Lawton State Bank illustrates the popularity of the postcard as a convenient means for communication, and in this case for advertising as well.

Buffalo on the Wichita Game Reserve, near Lawton, Okla.

40383-C-N

Like most of the southwest, Oklahoma is a land where the old exists alongside the new, the traditional along with the progressive. Almost on the eve of extinction, a few hundred buffalo were herded onto a number of Oklahoma game reserves where their numbers have since greatly appreciated. The Wichita Reserve outside of Lawton is an ideal location for these huge, wonderful creatures which once roamed through this area centuries before Europeans settled the New World.

The areas around Lawton have undeniable appeal: the beauty of the Wichita Mountains, Lake Lawtonka, the Holy City and Sunrise Easter Service, memorials at Fort Sill, and in Lawton itself, the Museum of the Great Plains. Before 1925, Lawton's Founder's Day Parade (now known as the Lawton Birthday and Rodeo Celebration) was its best known activity. Although the Easter Day Pageant has replaced it in the minds of many, the Founder's Celebration is still viewed with exhilaration and heart-swelling pride.

The first car of this 1913 motorcade with its flags, bunting, and patriotic motifs is graced with ladies protected by parasols.

Fire boys amusing the crowd with a water fight.
12th anniversary Celebration Lawton Okla. Bates.

This rare photo card is also from the 12th Annual Founder's Day Parade and festivities in August, 1913. Members of the Lawton Fire Department are spraying water on each another for the onlooking crowd's amusement.

Only an Oklahoman who has endured the Sooner States's blistering summers can fully appreciate the activity shown here. Respite from sun and wind are welcome and furnish an occasion for lighthearted frolic—just as this August water fight illustrates.

1901's 13 Anniversary Celebration Lawton, Okla. Bates.

The 13th annual celebration of Lawton's founding, shown here taking place in 1914, involved various civic, religious, and fraternal organizations. The women in this parade wear beautiful ornamental hats and capes which must have been very warm at mid-day in early August. Umbrellas held by spectators protect them from the glare and burn of the Oklahoma sun.

Today, festivities celebrating the city's founding include a rodeo, dances, races, and various contests.

As a long-time neighbor and economic contributor to Lawton, Fort Sill was represented in the Founder's Day celebrations and played a major role in the annual parade.

Mounted soldiers seen here proudly fly their colors and display their cannon. Note that the troops use both sides of this broad street. Since Fort Sill was a field artillery post, cannon were highly appropriate as a symbol of the nation's military forces.

Greer County Court House, Mangum, Okla.

The southeastern town of Mangum was once a part of Texas. In 1860, Texas Governor Sam Houston signed a reorganization bill recognizing the claim of the Lone Star State on the town. At this point, Indian Territory also made claims on the area.

Houston was an adopted son of John Rogers, an influential Cherokee Chief. After marrying Roger's daughter (Talahina or Diana), Houston gave up the governorship of Tennessee to join his adopted tribe as they moved into Indian Territory. When his wife died in 1833, Houston left Campbell (later renamed Gore) with a number of his Cherokee friends and headed south into what was later to become the state of Texas. The Indians returned, but Houston stayed to become the first Governor of the Republic and later, its first chief executive when it became a state.

Mangum was named for A. S. Mangum, the man who applied to the nascent Texas Republic for the land on which the town was later established. After 1880, the battle over who owned the land created considerable friction. The matter was finally settled in 1896 by the U. S. Supreme Court in favor of Oklahoma Territory.

Grant County Court House, Medford, Okla.

Situated along the old Chisholm Trail is the present-day town of Medford in north central Oklahoma. This area is one of the most productive wheat-growing regions in the United States. It has not been uncommon for farm boys who live to the south, east, and west of Medford to seek work in the area on both winter and summer wheat. The broad prairie land with its green, then brown crops gently swaying with Oklahoma breezes is a mosaic that few of them ever forget.

Oklahoma State Penitentiary, McAlester, Okla.

Many noteworthy people have been residents of the Oklahoma State Penitentiary, a forbidding structure sitting atop a hill in McAlester. Although some prisoners are on the prison farm which runs a dairy, the bulk of its prisoners are "in the walls." The institution is self-contained in concrete and brick with 14-foot high outside walls adding to an unfriendly appearance. The McAlester location was selected by the state legislature shortly after statehood was granted in 1907.

1A158-N

One of the activities which sets the McAlester Prison apart from other state penitentiaries is the annual prison rodeo. Carefully supervised to protect the spectators, the arrangement allows a number of the prisoners to engage in all the customary rodeo events, including bronc busting and steer wrestling. An event that was one of the more frightening contests—eventually discontinued—was the practice of attaching money (generally five to twenty dollars) to the horn of a bull and granting one of the inmates (a volunteer) the opportunity to obtain the cash any way he could.

Ten years before an act of Congress established the Indian Territory in 1830, the federal government signed a treaty with the Choctaw Nation ceding to them the land of present-day Pittsburg County where McAlester is located. The Choctaws did not make this area their residence before 1832, but Osages and other tribes inhabited it for many years before that date, in earth-covered, wood-framed houses in a dome shape.

The Chickasaws were also allocated acreage in this area in an 1833 treaty; their relationship with the Choctaws was friendly enough that no major problems occurred between the tribes. Less than a hundred years later, succeeding settlers built up Grand Avenue in McAlester.

Grand Avenue, McAlester, Okla.

First Presbyterian Church, McAlester, Okla.—8

Pittsburg County, where McAlester is situated, was named for the city in Pennsylvania. Both locations were rich in coal.

The discovery of coal led a man named J. J. McAlester to leave his home in Arkansas in the 1860's and head into Indian Territory. Beginning as a laborer on an ox team headed for Fort Sill, McAlester later learned the retail end of merchandising and, by the use of ingenuity and a glib tongue, was able to open his own tent store in 1869. Many of the town's residents accept this is the founding date of their community.

During J. J. McAlester's early days of seeking his fortune, he met and married Miss Rebecca Burney, sister of Ben Burney, who was later Governor of the Choctaw Nation. Though the Choctaws and Chickasaws were interrelated and McAlester could have sought favor from both tribes, he chose to accept citizenship with the Choctaw Nation.

"Samples" Coal Mine, McAlester, Okla.

The M. K. & T. Railroad, the first railroad in Indian Territory, ran its track alongside J. J. McAlester's store in 1872, and a post office was established on the site the following year. Though the spelling was wrong—it had one "l" too many—it was corrected in 1885 to the town's current name.

Four years later, in 1889, a more serious problem than the spelling arose. At that time, the Choctaw Coal and Railway Company (which became part of the Rock Island Line) offered to come to McAlester, but only if it received a $10,000 gratuity and all interests in the townsite. J. J. McAlester refused this offer, and the railroad located a mile further south where it founded its own town: South McAlester. The conflict was settled in court in J.J.'s favor, but final resolution did not occur until statehood in 1907. On May 10th, South McAlester became McAlester with the uniting of their post offices. The following day, however, the former McAlester became North McAlester, which created another mild stir.

McAlester High School, McAlester, Okla.

Italians came to McAlester during the late nineteenth century to work in the local coal mines. They brought with them their religion, work habits, social customs, and their cuisine. McAlester's Italians have maintained the authenticity of their cuisine; the results are not only for sale in local eateries, but are on display at the Annual Italian Festival which attracts visitors from all over the state.

In the shadow of Mount Scott outside Lawton, Lake Lawtonka has long been a paradise for boating enthusiasts, fishermen, and nature lovers. The lake itself is located next to Medicine Park, a popular recreation area. In 1940, the lake was over 1400 acres in size and served as the water supply for both Lawton and Fort Sill.

Lake Lawtonka, near Medicine Park, Okla.

Adjacent to the Wichita Mountains Wildlife Refuge, Lake Lawtonka is a perfect place to spend a quiet day. Protected animals of all sorts roam in their natural habitat.

The tourist boat "Passenger" was one of the first purely recreational vessels to ply the lake's waters. The faces of this group suggest that the idea was a popular one.

Originally called Jimtown because Jim happened to be the first name of four different local farmers, the town adopted the tribe name of the wife of one of the Jims after he established a post office in 1891. The Miami reservation was located nearby. The name was chosen particularly to honor Thomas Richardville, Chief of the Miamis, who was instrumental in securing legislation for the townsite's acquisition. Later, Northeastern Agricultural College was founded in Miami, and the town also became a center for the tri-state mining area. An armed forces air training station was built, providing revenue for the town along with the local cattle and dairy industries. Mining began here after 1905 when zinc and lead were discovered. Miami's proximity to the Grand Lake of the Cherokees has also been a positive factor for the area's economy, especially during the last few decades with large-scale developments for boaters, vacationers, and tourists.

Third Street,
Muskogee, Okla.

Most Oklahomans are unaware that for many years Muskogee was the second largest city in Oklahoma or that the prestigious University of Tulsa started in 1894 as a local Muskogee institution named Henry Kendall College.

The discovery of oil in the area, the vast acreage of fertile grasslands for cattle grazing, and the selection of the site as headquarters for the Dawes Commission contributed to the city's growth. The Dawes Commission was created in 1893 for the purpose of breaking up tribal relationships and dividing tribal holdings into individual 160-acre plots—or eighty acres for Indian minors.

Discovery of large pools of oil around Tulsa drew attention away from Muskogee and contributed to slowing the town's growth after 1920.

The Red River, separating Oklahoma from Texas, is perhaps the best known of Oklahoma's rivers, but the Arkansas River is not far behind in recognition. Muskogeeans have treasured it as their source for water and for some of the best fishing to be found anywhere. Catfish pulled from the river complimented with seasonal greens and buttered cornbread are a mouth-watering treat.

Traffic on the Arkansas River goes back many generations. First used by Indians in the area, its later users included river boats loading and delivering goods and pleasure boats providing scenic cruises.

ARKANSAS RIVER. MUSKOGEE. OKLA.   HAND COLORED

2B-H1328

The history of Muskogee can be traced to the early nineteenth century when naturalist Thomas Nuttall suggested in 1819 that the confluence of the Verdigris, Arkansas, and Neosho (Grand) Rivers would be an excellent location for a settlement. Early growth of Muskogee showed he was correct.

As with all of Oklahoma, Indians had always inhabited the area. After the Civil War numerous blacks, both those who had previously been slaves to the Indians and those recently freed from slavery in the South, began to farm and raise livestock at Muskogee. They were joined by other pioneers brought by the Missouri-Kansas-Texas Railroad which came through Muskogee in 1872. These newcomers represented a mixed lot: adventurers, homesteaders, legitimate businessmen, and entrepreneurs.

The Turner Hotel was one of Muskogee's finest and most popular accommodations. Another favorite was Sever's Hotel which featured "long beds for tall people."

The streetcar in front of the Turner belonged to the Muskogee Electric Traction Company, one of America's early municipal transportation systems.

TURNER HOTEL,
MUSKOGEE, OKLA.

SPAULDING COLLEGE, MUSKOGEE, OKLA.

H. B. Spaulding belonged to one of Muskogee's pioneer families. The institute bearing his name originally contained a kindergarten attended by many of the town's early youngster residents; classes were held in a room of Mrs. Mary Locke's home. The school became the Harrell International Institute before becoming Spaulding Institute. Mrs. Locke was the mother of Reverend Theo. Brewer, a Methodist minister, who was the Institute's first president.

Pictured here is Spaulding College.

Among Muskogee's outstanding features are its parks. At the turn of the century, Spaulding Park was a prominent picnic and recreation area, and as is seen here, the "Rustic Bridge" provided a good fishing place.

Rustic Bridge, Spaulding Park, Muskogee, Okla.—23

Bird's Eye View, Hyde Park, Muskogee, Okla.

Not unlike its namesake in London, Muskogee's Hyde Park was well planned and well used. It was developed with areas for musicians, playground and picnic areas, carefully tended foliage, manicured grounds, and gazebos. Hyde Park was regarded as more than just another place to throw pieces of bread to ducks.

In addition to this pleasant park, the Five Civilized Tribes Museum, the U.S.S. Batfish (a World War II submarine on exhibit), an antique car museum on Shawnee Bypass, and a reconstructed 19th-century army base near Fort Gibson are located in and around the community.

For several years, Muskogee was Oklahoma's most important city, where the Dawes Commission conducted much of its business and where relations between the Five Tribes and the U.S. Government were worked out. In August, 1905, the final plan for a separate Indian state to be called "Sequoyah" was devised, and justice was dispensed for the whole territory, including the newly opened Unassigned Lands in their first years.

The government handled much of this business at the Indian Agency Building. Built in the 1870's, it was converted into the Five Civilized Tribes Museum in 1965.

Old Indian Agency Building

Where the Government Transacted Business with the Indians for Years, Muskogee, Okla.

47

KATY HOTEL AND DEPOT,
MUSKOGEE, OKLA.

The Katy Hotel was not as large as the Turner or the Severs, but it was just as popular. "Katy" was the nickname of the Missouri-Kansas-Texas Railroad.

The depot became a famous landmark and a favored meeting place.

R. A. Patterson Residence, Muskogee, Okla.

Today, pioneer homes in Muskogee are few, and most early buildings have been destroyed, but there are exceptions. Among them are two homes of famous Oklahomans: the Patterson home and the Foreman residence which has been converted into a museum. Grant Foreman was an eminent Oklahoma historian. This card shows the sturdy structure which was the Patterson residence.

One of the more picturesque settings for an American college is outside Muskogee where Bacone College is located. It was built in 1880 by the Baptist Church to educate Indian children. One source states that the school began as the Baptist Mission House in Tahlequah and moved to its present site in 1885 because of Muskogee's importance to the Five Civilized Tribes. Bacone's grounds provided background in the movie about the life of the famous Indian athlete Jim Thorpe.

Besides being the oldest continuing college in Oklahoma, Bacone claims to be the first college established for the American Indian although it now accepts non-Indians. Professor Almon Bacone, an instructor at the Cherokee Male Seminary at Tahlequah, is credited as being the founder of the college.

Before the new Muskogee Central High School facility was built in the late 1960's as an integrated institution, black students generally attended separate schools. Dunbar School had been one of the black schools.

Field House, University of Oklahoma, Norman, Okla.

9A475-N

For reasons having more to do with football than with academics, the University of Oklahoma is more highly regarded than any other educational institution in the state. Bumper stickers which proclaim that "O.U. is Number 2" conclude with "God is Number 1" so that there is no mistaking priorities in the minds of many Oklahomans.

However, the University of Oklahoma is known as more than just another football school. O.U. has distinguished itself through its Department of Anthropology in animal research (particularly primate behavior), and also has well-regarded Departments of History, Agriculture, and Medicine.

O. U. was created by the First Territorial Legislature in 1890; 57 students were enrolled for the first classes September 15, 1892. It was decided that the university's architectural style should include several examples of collegiate Gothic. The Administration Building shown here is the third administration building; the other two facilities burned down. All three were built in an English medieval academic style.

Administration Building, University of Oklahoma, Norman, Okla.

105561-N

105559

This view of the university in its earlier years shows that some of the layout remains today as it was then. Since that time enrollment has grown manyfold and plenty of buildings have been added. Schools of medicine and law, a publishing division, and a crippled children's hospital are a few of the many additions.

Norman, home of the University of Oklahoma, was founded during the first Great Land Run in 1889. When bonds for constructing the university buildings sold below par, the citizens of Norman made up the $2,800 deficit. The Fine Arts Auditorium was built in the same general style as the third administration building seen in the previous card, with towers and medieval crenellations—an imposing style that reflected academic stability.

Fine Arts Auditorium, University of Oklahoma, Norman, Okla.

3371-29-N

51

4035 ENTRANCE, AUDITORIUM AND CHEMISTRY, UNIVERSITY OF OKLAHOMA, NORMAN, OKLA.

In its early architectural homogeneity, even the entrance to the university employed towers and arches. This scene gives a different perspective of the Fine Arts Auditorium, Chemistry Building and gateway from the two previous postcards. The wide parkway leading to the school was donated by two residents of Norman, and became University Boulevard.

Public School, Nowata, Okla.

The site of Nowata, originally on Cherokee land, was sold by this tribe to the Kansas Delaware Indians in 1868. A small community grew out of a trading post on the site. It was later named Nowata, although the source and interpretation of the name are open to question. The surrounding territory includes farming and ranch land in addition to picturesque Oolagah Lake.

Presbyterian Church, Nowata, Okla.

This Presbyterian Church in Nowata features a massive bell tower with louvres which indicate that bells were housed inside and were meant to be heard. The architect used an interesting combination of square forms and arched window tops.

EISCHEN'S (ANTIQUE) BAR—OLDEST IN OKLAHOMA—OKARCHE, OKLA.

The fact that this is an advertising card is borne out by the story of the bar on the card's reverse. The bar was originally built in Spain in the early to mid-1800's; the carver's family crest appears on each of its pillars. During the gold rush days, the bar was shipped to California. Finding at least one other home after its trip to the West Coast, the bar finally arrived in Okarche as the property of Jack Eischen.

City Market, Oklahoma City, Okla.

Before the Land Run of April 22, 1889, Oklahoma City was known simply as Oklahoma Station—a stop along the Sante Fe Railroad. The town's citizens claim that it is the only city in history to be born in a single afternoon. By the night of April 22nd, almost 10,000 people had laid claim to land in what would become inside the city limits.

More than two decades after the run, this 1910 scene shows a bustling town teeming with activity—"busting at the seams," as some of those early folks might have bragged. Oklahoma City started with a mad rush and continued in that vein for several decades; it accelerated politically and culturally in an explosion of economic progress.

In the period bewteen the Land Rush and the time that the United States Congress sanctioned the incorporation of Oklahoma City, some citizens plotted the townsite and provided local government. But a like-minded group took the same course of action in another part of town. The result was that two different survey companies established conflicting boundaries and street layouts, one on the north side; one on the south.

The north-south problem was finally resolved, but too late to prevent Walker Street jogging at Sheridan. The original plotting occurred north and south of Clarke Street, which later became Grand Avenue as seen here. The name was changed once more to Sheridan.

Grand Ave., East from Harvey St., Oklahoma City, Okla.—25

Main Street, Looking East, Oklahoma City, Okla.

Like most other towns across America, Oklahoma City had a "Main Street." As indicated by this 1940's scene, Main Street in Oklahoma's capital was a busy thoroughfare.

Oklahoma City's love affair with the automobile reached the point where the level of pedestrian traffic was much lower than in most cities of similar size. It is not surprising that Oklahoma City is the home of the parking meter.

First National Bank Building seen on the right has been considered to be one of the most magnificent structures in the state. Italian marble flooring on the second level with beautiful murals and reproductions of ancient coins decorating the walls combine to create a true showplace. The petroleum building on the left features an oil well derrick on the top.

2B-H864

This aerial view in the 1940's or 1950's shows the business center of Oklahoma City. During this period, proper downtown attire meant gloves, hats and high heels for women and business suits for men. Long after New York, Chicago, and Los Angeles had decreed that informal wear was appropriate, Oklahoma City's downtown population maintained its elegant, formal style of dress.

To accommodate the increasing diversity of its population and the changing tastes of society in general, millions of dollars were spent in Oklahoma City on new governmental and cultural facilities and better accommodations for both entertainers on tour and business groups seeking a haven. The Civic Auditorium, which gave way to the Myriad Convention Center, was such a municipal improvement.

CIVIC AUDITORIUM, OKLAHOMA CITY, OKLA.

CIVIC AUDITORIUM

6A-H2686

1401. Epworth University, Oklahoma City, Oklahoma.

Epworth University was begun by the Methodist Church in 1904, and was located on the site of the Epworth Methodist Church outside of town.

It was merged with Fort Worth University in 1911, removed to Guthrie, and renamed the Methodist University of Oklahoma. Its last move occurred in 1919 when it returned to Oklahoma City as Oklahoma City University.

After the university was moved in 1919, O.C.U. began a period of expansion. By 1957 the school had 4,000 students and was accredited by the North Central Association of Colleges and Universities.

An evening college was added in 1922, and its medical school merged with the University of Oklahoma in 1910.

OKLAHOMA CITY UNIVERSITY, OKLAHOMA CITY, OKLA.—40

Sadly, few cities in America have retained their original courthouses even as historic sites. Outgrown buildings are frequently torn down and replaced. As seen here, Oklahoma City's early courthouse was not especially large, but it was a solid structure of Richardson Romanesque style. These brick or limestone buildings were built to endure.

COURT HOUSE, OKLAHOMA CITY, OKLA.

During its early years, Oklahoma City was very much a western town where large, excellent breakfasts and comfortable accommodations were provided by hotels like the Threadgill.

Note that all the windows on what must be the west side of the hotel have awnings to protect rooms from the hot afternoon sun.

1402. Threadgill Hotel, Oklahoma City, Oklahoma.

Stock Yards Scene, Oklahoma City, Okla.—41

Meat packing is a major industry for Oklahoma City, and stock yards represent an important element in this industry. The most distinctive section of Oklahoma City was "Packing Town."

The Baptist White Temple, Oklahoma City, Okla.

The earliest missions to Indian tribes in Oklahoma were sponsored by Methodists, Presbyterians, and Baptists. Today these demoninations are still in Oklahoma, but Baptists outnumber the others by a wide margin here and in the neighboring states of Texas and Arkansas as well. Some of the Baptist churches were stately edifices like the Baptist White Temple, built in a classical style, but most were less pretentious and, in the beginning, of modest wooden frame construction.

The list of things to see in Oklahoma City includes Oklahoma Heritage Center, Enterprise Square, National Cowboy Hall of Fame, 45th Infantry Division Museum, Oklahoma Art Center, Kirkpatrick Center, Oklahoma Firefighters Museums, Oklahoma Museum of Art, Frontier City, and the National Softball Hall of Fame.

O'Mealey's
CAFETERIA
319-21 N. W. 23rd STREET
OKLAHOMA CITY

Anyone who ever ate a meal at one of Oklahoma City's O'Mealey's cafeterias will remember the experience as a pleasurable one.

The dining rooms were comfortable and clean with a simple elegance that belied the word "cafeteria." O'Mealey's home cooking appealed to a large slice of Oklahoma's population.

The author worked in the O'Mealey's located on 23rd, down from the capital, and enjoyed the compliments of state senators about the cornbread and rolls that he prepared daily.

When Oklahoma still belonged to the Indians, The Sante Fe was among the first of the large railroads to build through the territory. Other railroads were the Missouri-Kansas-Texas (Katy); the Atlantic and Pacific Company which ran a line to Sapulpa as early as 1886; the Rock Island (Chicago, Rock Island and Pacific), and the Frisco (St. Louis and San Francisco). The last two railroads were served by the fine terminal shown here.

UNION STATION, OKLAHOMA CITY, OKLA.

4A-H323

Oklahoma City Golf and Country Club, Oklahoma City, Okla.

Hunting and fishing aren't the only sports in Oklahoma, as this card makes amply clear.

The stately colonial-style Governor's Mansion has a working oil well on the grounds, which seems appropriate since oil plays a major role in the Sooner state's economy.

GOVERNOR'S MANSION, OKLAHOMA CITY, OKLA.—41

The Oklahoma State Capitol building is reminiscent of the nation's capitol building in Washington, D. C., except for a dome. This building has no dome for a very practical reason: the money ran out. The building as it stands today was completed in 1917, but the dome issue is not dead—from time to time serious consideration has been given to adding the dome.
On the capital grounds are a number of oil derricks operated by different oil companies.

The Civic Center, completed in 1937, was the former site of a railroad switching yard. Joseph Overton Paar, noted as one of America's foremost architects, designed the building.

Civic Center by Night, Oklahoma City, Okla.

OIL FIELD
OKLAHOMA CITY, OKLA.—47

The oil boom in Oklahoma City began in 1928, but it was the Mary Sudik Gusher of 1930 that created the real furor. The Sudik sprayed its black treasure all the way to Norman, 15 miles away. Over 30,000 barrels spewed from the geyser in all directions for eleven days.

Of the parks and recreational areas constructed by Oklahoma City, Belle Isle was always a favorite thanks to its pleasant walkways, gazebo, and view of the lake. Another popular attraction, especially during the 1950's and 1960's, was Spring Lake, where top names in the music business made guest appearances.

Views of Belle Isle,
Oklahoma City, Okla.

CLARA H. GIRVIN BRIDGE,
LINCOLN PARK,
OKLAHOMA CITY, OKLA.—22

Oklahoma City's former Lincoln Park has one of the nation's largest and most prestigious zoos. Exotic animals are seen in their natural settings as one follows zigzagging trails. The facility has expanded in the past few decades; by 1940 Lincoln Park was 540 acres in size and offered, besides its world-famous zoo, facilities for bowling, fishing, golfing, picnicking, boating, and swimming.

The bridge in this picture was named in 1923 for Clara Girvin, the first woman to serve on the Oklahoma City Park Board.

WHEELER PARK, HORIZONTAL GROWING TREE, OKLAHOMA CITY, OKLA.

Wheeler Park was the first of its kind built in Oklahoma City and was very popular for many years. During the early years of the twentieth century, vaudeville acts, a skating rink, a magic mirror parlor, and a miniature railroad competed with the beautiful zoological gardens, lawns, and tree-lined walking paths for the attention of its visitors.

The park epitomized "Sunday in the park" at a time when that phrase carried its most pleasant connotations.

A RESTFUL CORNER OF THE LOBBY

A CORNER OF THE ROSE DINING ROOM

These views show the glamour of Oklahoma City's Hotel Black during the middle decades of this century. The interior was both plush and comfortable. This hotel was selected by army recruiters to house volunteers and inductees when these men were sent to the city for their routine physical examinations.

Creek Council House, Okmulgee, Okla.

Okmulgee was previously known as the Creek Indian Capital. In 1868, the Creeks moved their tribal headquarters from Council Hill to Okmulgee where they built a new council house. In 1870 Okmulgee was the site of an important meeting of the Five Civilized Tribes to discuss unification and possible establishment of a separate Indian state. The Indians feared was what was already in process: lands in the western part of the territory were being parcelled out to various out-of-state tribes as punishment for the Oklahoma Indians' affiliation with the Confederacy during the Civil War. The Five Tribes predicted that all their tribal holdings would eventually be taken from them piece-meal; this is exactly what the Dawes Commission was empowered to do.

The city of Okmulgee dates itself from 1899 when the Creek communal holdings were broken into individual lots. The old Creek Council House is now a museum of fascinating Indian artifacts.

PARKINSON HOTEL, OKMULGEE, OKLA.

The name of the city is taken from the Creek words *oki mulgi* meaning "boiling waters" or "bubbling water." The parked cars, the mailbox, and the utility poles in front of the Parkinson Hotel are indicative of Okmulgee's progress from its Indian days to an oil industry town where glass manufacturing and pecan production have also added to the economic base.

Aerial View, Part of Down-town, Okmulgee, Okla.

OC-H864

One advantage of attending eight schools in eight school districts was the opportunity for the author to live in a number of Oklahoma towns. One of them was Okmulgee.

In the mid-1950's A & M Technical College was a familiar landmark that permitted fishing in the lake adjacent to it. In 1956, the latest architectural additions were Horace Mann Grammar School and a Dairy Queen on Wood Drive that dispensed five-cent cones filled with ice cream which tasted as good on the fingers and the back of the hand as it did when licked from the cone.

This is Okmulgee's early country club, owner of this extended bungalow-style clubhouse building. This view shows several large chimneys indicative of fireplaces, a porch, and a broad expanse of windows. Under the eaves of the gabled roof extensions, brackets are used in an unusual way, and attic windows are hooded in an attractive manner.

Home of the nation's first Boy Scout troop which was organized in 1909, Pawhuska is also the headquarters of the Osage Nation, richest of all the Indian tribes.

The town itself is Osage, named after Chief Paw-Hiu-Skah, whose name means "white hair." The chief was leader of the Osages at the turn of the century and presided when the tribe split into two factions. This schism is thought to have happened when Paw-Hiu-Skah assumed the position of chief in violation of tribal law.

Osage Indian Agency, Pawhuska, Okla.

A member of the Osage tribe with international reputation was Maria Tallchief, one of the greatest ballerinas in the world.

The Osage Trail Museum and the Osage County Historical Museum are located in Pawhuska. Among Pawhuska's former residents was President Herbert Hoover, who spent several boyhood summers here with an uncle who was an Osage agent.

Established in September, 1893, when the Cherokee Outlet was opened for settlement, Perry had trouble in the early days keeping the peace, and three U. S. Marshals were sent to quiet things down until a local government could be organized. The post office was established in Perry on August 25, 1893. Named for J. A. Perry who was a member of the Cherokee Strip Commission during President Grover Cleveland's administration, Perry serves as the county seat for Noble County.

Spacious and Modern Post Office — Federal Building at Perry, Oklahoma

Prize Winner, Flower Parade, Perry, Okla.

After a boisterous beginning, Perry settled down to become a prosperous community where some of the industries have been flour milling, dairy-products processing, cement manufacturing, sheet- metal products, leather, pottery, and oil production. The local people take time off for the Annual Cherokee Outlet Celebration, and as we see here, to compete, years ago, in the Flower Parade.

Picher owes its early life and name to the mining industry. Named after W. S. Picher of the Eagle-Picher Lead Company, the Picher post office was established June 2, 1916. The town is a center in the lead- and zinc-mining area which extends into Kansas and Missouri, and has been the headquarters for mining companies, smelters, and refineries, and for makers of mining machinery and equipment.

H-1943 PICHER LEAD AND ZINC MILLS, PICHER, OKLA. (MIAMI DISTRICT.)

Wentz Boy Scout Swimming Pool is still in operation, but under the city department of parks. This tranquil scene pictured beyond a patch of daisies does not give a hint of the sad story of the Indians for whom the town was named.

After ceding land to the Poncas in a show of good faith, the U.S. Government reconsidered the treaty in light of developments involving the fierce Sioux tribesmen. Wishing to placate the Sioux, the earlier arrangement with the Poncas was disregarded, and the Poncas were to be relocated in 1877 to the eastern part of Indian Territory. The forced march was the Poncas' "Trail of Tears" —not unlike that endured by the Cherokees and other tribes on their way west.

Included among the 30% who died of starvation, disease, and exposure on the march was the teenage son of Ponca chief, Standing Bear. The youth's last request was to be buried in his ancestral home. To comply with this wish, Standing Bear began the trek back with those Poncas who wished to accompany him. They stopped temporarily at the reservation of their near-kinsmen in Nebraska, the Omahas. There they were placed under arrest and marched to the fort at Omaha from where they would be returned to Indian Territory as renegades and outlaws. The chief, still carrying his son's bones, could only comply.

WENTZ BOY-SCOUT SWIMMING POOL, PONCA CITY, OKLA.

The tragedy of the Ponca Indians came to the attention of a newspaper reporter named Thomas Tibbles who wrote of the Indians' plight in the *Omaha Herald*. His article was read by the Susette LaFlesche, the daughter of an Omaha Chief; she devoted the next several years to lecturing and writing on behalf of the Poncas and other dispossessed, ill-treated Indians.

The results of her efforts were mixed. Standing Bear and his group were allowed to return to their homeland, but those Poncas still in Oklahoma were forced to remain there.

The attire seen in this 1911 picture taken near Ponca City illustrates the situation of the Indian people caught between two cultures.

Part of the Cherokee Outlet opening in 1893, Ponca City progressed from prairie grass to city in one September afternoon.

A government map indicated that the town was to be named "Cross," but the first citizens had different ideas, and not only about the name—they also preferred a town site closer to the Ponca Indian reservation. The railroad refused to comply, but the problem was eventually resolved when Cross was annexed to Ponca City after the latter town grew to the smaller community's city limits.

Continental Oil Co. Office Building, Ponca City, Okla.

HARVEY PHOTO

7A408-N

Before 1910, cattle ranching and farming competed with the oil business to form the foundation of Ponca City's economy. From about 1910 until just before 1940, E. W. Marland employed many of Ponca City's citizens and served as the city's benefactor. Unquestionably one of the most successful oil wild-catters of all time, Marland became a legend.

Within a few years of obtaining an agreement with a Ponca Chief permitting him to drill into an Indian burial ground, Marland owned 600 service stations and conducted his petroleum business in seventeen foreign countries and every state in the Union. In one day, he gave almost $2,500,000 to the Osage Tribe. Marland himself lived the oil baron's lifestyle on a 400-acre estate in Ponca City.

Marland went into politics and successfully ran for the U.S. Congress. Meanwhile, his oil business declined, and he was bought out by J. P. Morgan in 1927 when oil prices plummeted. Almost broke by the following year, the undaunted Marland ran for governor, was elected, and governed quite successfully.

He permitted the drilling of oil wells near the Executive Mansion, which displeased some people but augmented the state's coffers. He died in 1941 in poverty.

71

Pioneer Woman Statue, Ponca City, Okla.

HARVEY PHOTO   7A410-N

Twelve noted sculptors competed for the Pioneer Woman statue commission sponsored by E. W. Marland. People voted for their favorite entry, and Bryant Baker's entry won. Unveiled on April 22, 1930, the bronze sculpture was dedicated by Will Rogers.

Holding her child's hand and clutching her Bible, the woman represents, in Marland's words, the "best and bravest women, who became the unknown soldiers in the great battle for civilization and homesteads . . . . With this monument, I hope to preserve for the children the story of our mothers' fight and toil and courage." The statue was given to the state of Oklahoma; it stands in front of the Pioneer Woman Museum which was dedicated in 1958.

The author remembers his mother dressing very much like this, which did not prevent her from hauling hay, picking cotton, beans, and strawberries, or swinging a forceful wooden "switch" on any of her brood who needed disciplining.

Before the height requirement was changed, this hill outside Poteau was considered a mountain. After the change, it took its rightful place of prominence as the "world's highest hill." Its height is 1,999 feet.

World's Highest Hill

Pryor, Okla. After the Tornado. 6

Lying on a broad stretch of flatland, Pryor—like much of the rest of the state—is without natural defenses against the fury of Oklahoma's frequent tornados. The twister responsible for the damage depicted here occurred on April 22, 1942. Again like other Oklahoma communities, the city was rebuilt on a grander scale than the original town fathers had ever envisioned.

Named for Nathaniel Pryor, one of the scouts with the Lewis and Clark Expedition, the town was settled in 1872 on the site of an old trading post, and has become a center for manufacturing. One of Pryor's main attractions is the Coo-Y-Yah Museum, a repository of many interesting pioneer items.

As a stop along the Atchison, Topeka and Sante Fe Railway, Purcell's history preceded the 1889 Run by almost two years. Although the town was named for the engineer who surveryed the region for the railroad, its history is decidedly Indian. This area belonged to the Chickasaw nation, but other tribes lived and hunted here, especially before 1880. The area is rich in Indian lore and is worth exploring for its historical interest. Noted for raising cotton, Purcell built a cotton gin to process its own crops.

Purcell's Elks Lodge building is pictured in this postcard; note that an artist has carefully removed utility lines wherever possible to enhance the beauty of the scene.

B. P. O. Elks No. 1260, Purcell, Okla.

This generic Oklahoma card sends embossed greetings from Rush Springs, home of the annual Watermelon Festival. Just about every variety of watermelon is grown in the Sooner State—Cobb Jim, Irish Grey, Congo, Tom Watson (and improved variations), Mountain Hoosier, and the gigantic Black Diamond are among them. These and other varieties are put on display at Rush Springs where free slices are generously provided. Carnivals, parades, watermelon-seed-spitting contests, and watermelon judging are included in the annual August festivities.

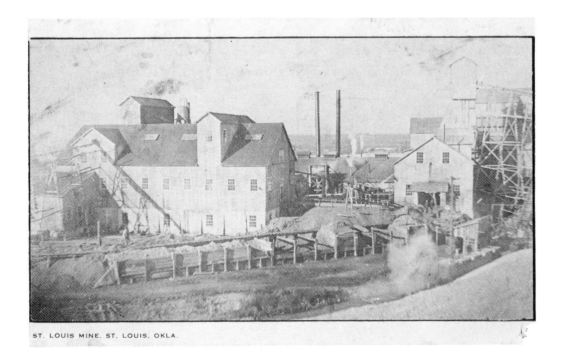

ST. LOUIS MINE. ST. LOUIS, OKLA.

The mining operation pictured here suggests a larger population than the 109 souls listed by the 1980 census. St. Louis, located in a mainly agricultural part of the State, was named for the large city in Missouri. A post office was established in 1928 around the time of the town's popularity peak. Like many other western mining towns, the population has dwindled.

This rare photo postcard of Sharon, Oklahoma, shows a community along the railroad right-of-way that could easily be missed if one were to blink a couple of times. Formerly known as Hackberry, the post office name was changed to Sharon in 1912, recognizing Alexander Sharon, the townsite's owner. It's an area for production of livestock and grain.

In 1850, James Sapulpa of the Creek Indian tribe moved from Alabama to the area later named for his family. By 1886, the Atlantic and Pacific Railroad, which became the St. Louis and San Francisco Railway Company (The Frisco), had run track from St. Louis to Sapulpa. By July of 1889 a post office had been established. Construction on this handsome high school began February 10, 1918, with the cost for completion estimated at $179,872. Torn down in 1968, the site was home to a variety store, and now serves as the location for a grocery store.

BERRYHILL BUILDING, SAPULPA, OKLA.

The Earle Berryhill Building at 18 E. Dewey was completed in 1909. According to the plaque on the building, the "Headright oil income of Earle, Creek Roll No. NB 988 (a minor) was utilized as an investment for him by his father Theodore, C. R. No. 2519 (son of George W.)." The Berryhills, one of the richest of the Creek Indian families, benefited from the Glenn Pool oil strike of Novermber 22, 1905. The Glenn Pool oilfield at that time was the largest oil field in the world. Of particular interest is the brickwork of the facade. The building is still standing.

World-famous Frankoma pottery is made in Sapulpa. John Frank, founder of the company, had taught ceramic art at Oklahoma University in Norman, and was on his way to start a factory in Kansas when his car broke down in Sapulpa. Stopping in a local coffee shop, he was convinced by the owner to stay in Sapulpa.

The Stillwater area was part of the original Unassigned Lands where Boomers unsuccessfully attempted to settle in 1884. Stillwater was selected as a registration point for the 1893 opening of the Cherokee Outlet and was settled in 1889.

This early view with its broad dirt street looks like a set for a western movie. The flagpole shown in this card apparently was "enhanced" by an artist; the pole was maintained by the post office at the corner of Seventh and Main to advise citizens of the weather forecast. Each day a telegram came from the weather bureau in Oklahoma City, and a set of flags was flown from the pole in accordance with this information. Merchants along the street gave out cards listing flag meanings.

MAIN STREET, STILLWATER, OKLA.

In addition to the American flag which seems to be painted on as an afterthought, the car driving down the street is obviously the work of a paint brush rather than the camera.

Stillwater's current attractions include the Museum of Natural and Cultural History; Sheerar Cultural and Heritage Museum with its excellent display of antique photos and American china, glass, and buttons; the Museum of Higher Education in Oklahoma; National Wrestling Hall of Fame; and the Fred Pfeiffer Collection of antique farm equipment.

76

Student Union Building, Oklahoma State University
Stillwater, Oklahoma

Approximately a year and a half after Stillwater was founded, the Territorial Legislature established there a college of agriculture, called Oklahoma Agricultural and Mechanical College (Oklahoma A & M). The college attained university status in 1957; in the 1988-89 school year seven percent of the student body was enrolled in the College of Agriculture.

The Student Union, constructed in 1950, houses an 81-room hotel, a theatre, several lounges, meeting rooms, a post office, a travel agency, dining areas, and several university offices within its 543,400 square feet of space. The Union is the site of many campus activities.

Harry Cordell at one time was president of the Oklahoma Board of Agriculture, and a friend of education who convinced the 13th legislature to approve the sale of building bonds for development of higher educational facilities. The building shown here and Willard Hall were financed through these bonds, and to honor the man whose interest and leadership capabilities benefited the school, Cordell Hall was named for him. Originally a residence hall for 576 male students, it now houses offices. When built, it was acclaimed for having one of the largest and most efficient kitchens in any facility of its type in the nation.

Cordell Hall, A. & M. College, Stillwater, Okla.

Judging from the automobiles in the background, this card was probably produced in the mid thirties. These Indian dancers on a Stillwell street model ceremonial costumes adorned with feathers and bells, reflecting traditions of longer endurance than car styles.

A Cherokee mission was organized in this area in the early 1800's by Dr. Marcus Palmer.

Stillwell claims the title "Strawberry Capital of the World" and celebrates annually with a strawberry festival in May. The success of strawberry horticulture is demonstrated by this slightly exaggerated photograph. Oversized plants and creatures have frequently been the subject of postcards; giant Idaho potatoes, monstrous Louisiana crayfish, and ears of corn from Iowa the size of barrels are typical of this means of community self-aggrandizement.

Not only are the strawberry crops bountiful in Stillwell, Adair county, but the fishing is wonderful, too. Both of these Adair county postcards are the work of the same humorist.

Caught In Adair
Photo By Clark

Sulphur, Oklahoma, is known for Platt National Park and its mineral water, a principal tourist attraction. The park and the Arbuckle Recreation Area are now combined in the Chickasaw National Recreation Area.

Underground wells provide Sulphur's water supply and also fill the town's many swimming pools. Outside of town in the recreation area are multiple springs with mineral contents ranging from sulphur to bromide and iron. The Vendome Well is among the world's largest flowing mineral springs.

VENDOME ARTESIAN WELL, PLATT NATIONAL PARK, SULPHUR, OKLA.

100420

NURSES QUARTERS, TALIHINA INDIAN HOSPITAL, TALIHINA, OKLA.

Before the railroad put in its appearance, Talihina (which means "Iron Road" in Choctaw) was an unidentified missionary settlement on most maps. The settlement prospered when the Frisco railroad came in 1888, although it remained small. Talihina is located near the western extremity of the Quachita National Forest in southeastern Oklahoma. Because of its remoteness, Talihina has been a favored spot of hunters, fishermen, campers, and wildlife enthusiasts.

The sanitarium was built in 1921 when the favored treatment for tuberculosis was rest in an outdoor environment. The hospital is now operated by the state as the Talihina Veterans Center; it's located about a mile away from the Indian Hospital in the next card.

MEN'S BUILDING
EASTERN OKLAHOMA STATE SANITARIUM, TALIHINA, OKLAHOMA

One of the more positive governmental actions on behalf of the American Indian has been the establishment of hospitals. This hospital at Talihina was opened in 1938 and originally had 225 beds, primarily for Indians who suffered from tuberculosis. After new cures for TB were found, surgery and obstetrics became the main areas of focus. Since February of 1985, the hospital has been maintained by the Choctaw tribe with federal funds, and is now named the Choctaw Nation Indian Hospital. The former nurses' quarters now house those who take part in the Indian Health Service training program provided by the federal government. The tile roofs are still in place.

80

This north-central Oklahoma community was named for the Tonkawa Indians whose name has been interpreted to mean "they all stay together". They wandered the plains from Texas northward, remaining inseparable.

In 1879 Chief Joseph and his followers of the Nez Perce tribe were brought to this area by the U. S. Cavalry and placed on a reservation at the Yellow Bull crossing. The area of Tonkawa lies within the Cherokee Outlet and was opened for white settlement when the Cherokee Outlet Land Run took place in 1893. This photo card shows the Tonkawa University Preparatory School and Junior College, established in 1901.

Since the early years of the twentieth century, Tulsa has been as active and fast-paced as this picture suggests. The city started as a post office on a pony mail route through the Creek Nation in 1879, about the same time that the Atlantic and Pacific Railroad began using it as a loading station for shipping cattle to large stockyards.

Tulsey (or Tulsee) Town was its original name and is still occasionally used with affection today. The name came from the Creek Indians (the Lochapokas) who were originally part of the Tallassee Community of Alabama. Their first residence in Oklahoma was along the lower Arkansas and Verdigris Rivers, but they finally moved to the vicinity of Tulsa.

"The Best"

THE MAYO — TULSA

Early milestones in Tulas's history include a French trader, Bernard De La Harpe, who came within thirty miles of the future city in 1719, Washington Irving, who visited the area briefly in 1832, and Creek Indian Archie Yahola who came upon the site of Tulsa in 1836, the same year that the Creeks built a council fire here after their tragic journey west over the "Trail of Tears."

Decades later when Tulsa had become a commercial center, hotels made arrival in Tulsa more comfortable. The Mayo Hotel, as someone has written on the front of this card, was "The Best"—not just in Tulsa, but in the whole southwest, according to a lot of people. The hotel was built in two stages; the second stage comprised the upper half.

The Mayo family who built this hotel were socially prominent in Tulsa and were benefactors to the city. Unlike many well-to-do people in the area, they made their money in hotels and office buildings, not oil.

In 1989, the hotel stood empty.

The Alvin Hotel did not command the same respect as the Mayo, but it does hold the distinction of having the Society for the Preservation and Encouragement of Barber Shop Quartet Singing in America organized here over half a century ago.

The ALVIN   Seventh and Main
TULSA, OKLAHOMA

82

BOSTON AVENUE
METHODIST CHURCH

TULSA, OKLAHOMA
ONP-3

Tulsans who lived here during the 1940's through the 1960's will recognize this view. Boston Avenue is one of the main streets of the downtown area.

ONC-26— Boston Avenue, Looking North, Tulsa, Oklahoma

The Boston Avenue Methodist Church is an impressive landmark, and undoubtedly one of the five most outstanding Art Deco buildings in the USA.

Originally the creative concept of local artist Adah Robinson, responsibility for the design as executed is disputed by Adah's student, Bruce Goff, who claimed it for himself.

The limestone walls of the building's illuminated tower rise 225 ft., adorned with bas relief portraits of pioneers including Methodist itinerant preachers who came to Oklahoma in the early days, and other figures important in Methodism such as John Wesley.

The pre-eminent example of Art Deco style in Tulsa which is known for its Art Deco architecture, the church was finished in 1929.

Rose Garden, Woodward Park, Tulsa, Okla.

Tulsa's Municipal Rose Garden has won awards ever since it was established in 1934. Notable awards were given in 1937 by *Better Homes and Gardens* magazine, and in 1979 by the American Rose Society for the "Most Outstanding Rose Garden, South Central District" by the American Rose Society in 1979. Certificates and plaques throughout the 33.9-acre garden document many other awards from over the years. Over 278 varieties of roses are represented in almost 9,000 plantings. The garden has been featured in many garden books and since 1945 has been the site of an All-American Rose Society Test Garden.

The author was fortunate to have lived in the city during the first year of his marriage and can recall the many visits he made to this place with his lovely bride.

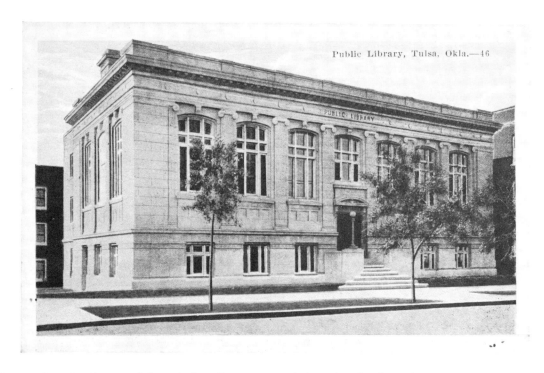

Public Library, Tulsa, Okla.—46

This Tulsa Public Library building, a gift from Andrew Carnegie, was dedicated in October, 1915, according to the cornerstone which has been incorporated into the ramp for handicapped people at the Tulsa County Historical Society Museum, located in the renovated Thomas Gilcrease House. The library building was torn down years ago and the location is now a parking lot.

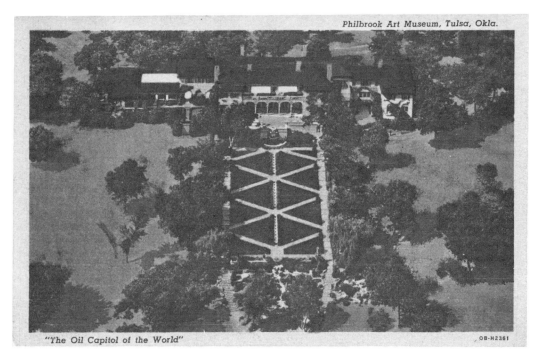

"The Oil Capitol of the World"   OB-H2361

Philbrook was originally the residence of oil baron Waite Phillips, brother of the Woolaroc Museum creator and philanthropist, Frank Phillips. Both brothers collected art and Western artifacts, competing with each other to Oklahoma's eventual advantage. Waite's collection is housed in the Italian Renaissance-style mansion built in 1926 and set in 23 acres of formal gardens. Philbrook houses an impressive collection of American Indian art, Italian Renaissance paintings and sculpture, and other collections.

Another very important art collection is also located in Tulsa in the Gilcrease Museum which was once the home of millionaire Thomas Gilcrease. The museum is also among the finest repositories in the world for the works of Frederic Remington, Thomas Moran, Charles Russell, and George Catlin. Gilcrease had collected over 10,000 works of art, 50,000 American artifacts, and 90,000 rare books and documents.

Mounting debt eventually forced Gilcrease to sell his museum and its collection. In 1954, wishing to retain his valuable collection in Tulsa, citizens of the city passed a bond issue which covered Gilcrease's debts and purchased both the home and the collection. Gilcrease is buried on the grounds.

The Tulsa County Historical Society Museum is located in the Gilcrease mansion.

ONC-29— Mid-Continent Oil Refinery and Skyline of Tulsa, Okla.

OB-H2362

After the discovery of oil in Red Fork in 1901, Tulsa became the "Oil Capital of the World." During the first five decades of this century many companies directly or indirectly related to the petroleum industry established Tulsa as their base of operations. By 1988 1,000 oil and oil-related companies had established headquarters or outlets in the city.

85

ONC-19—Skelly Stadium, University of Tulsa, Okla.

DELMER L. CURTIS-AERIAL PHOTO SERVICE   8B-H411

Skelly Stadium, home of Tulsa University's "Golden Hurricane" football team, originally seated 14,500, but was expanded in 1947 when 5,000 seats were added in the north end. By 1958 the seating capacity had become too limited and in 1965 the stadium was renovated and expanded, and a press box was added. It now seats 44,210.

The stadium was named after oil man William Skelly who donated $125,000 to the stadium fund in 1930; the other $175,000 was raised by Tulsa businessmen. Ground breaking took place May 11, 1930.

Bird Creek Falls was a favorite picnic location around the turn of the century, but no longer enjoys the same fame. It is located in the north end of town.

Bird Creek Falls, near Tulsa, Okla.

FIRST METHODIST CHURCH, VINITA, OKLA.

Vinita began in 1871 when the Missouri Kansas-Texas Railroad and the Atlantic and Pacific Railway interrupted their rivalry long enough to form a junction in this area.

The town's name came from Vinnie Ream, sculptress of the life- size statue of Abraham Lincoln in Washington, D.C. One of Vinita's important early citizens who was also a Cherokee Indian, Colonel Elias C. Boudinot, chose the town's name. A community established on the site in 1870 (Downingville) was absorbed by Vinita.

Vinita and the surrounding area are famous for its fishing and hunting. The Brangus cattle, a hornless mixed breed of Brahma and Aberdeen-Angus, is raised here on prime grazing land. Vinita also hosts the Will Rogers Memorial Rodeo, held in August. The rodeo was first held in 1935; Rogers was to have been the guest of honor, but he died in an airplane crash at Point Barrow, Alaska, with his pilot friend Wiley Post with whom he had embarked on a what was to be a globe-circling flight. The famous cowboy attended secondary school in Vinita.

COURT HOUSE, VINITA, OKLAHOMA

SCENE ON CAPITOL HILL, WAURIKA, OKLA.

Called Monika by the railroad when it established a station here in 1892, the town was renamed Waurika, an adaptation of an Indian word meaning "pure water." A post office was established here in 1902. Waurika Lake, a U. S. Army Corps of Engineers project, is located nearby.

Woodward County Court House,
Woodward, Okla.

The Court House in this picture served Woodward County from 1902 to 1937, but as early as 1919 the need for a new one was being discussed. After 1937 the building was used for other purposes until 1947 when a tornado swept through the Woodward area and severely damaged the building to the extent that it was necessary to demolish it completely. The tornado had a girth of two and a half miles and holds the record (as of this writing) for devastation in Oklahoma.

Woodward is part of the Cherokee Strip area, and was not officially settled before the 1893 Run. However, when the Run took place, there were a lot of buildings to run around in Woodward, including a railroad depot. Prior to the Run, supposedly only railroad and government people were living there, but Woodward celebrated its centennial in 1987.

"Old Central" High School was used from 1911 to 1929; the new one built in 1929 has since been superceded by another new school built in 1978. Old Central no longer stands.

The town was a recipient of a Carnegie Library building which is still standing as of this writing, but which has been outgrown. In August, 1988, the old post office became the new library.

Woodward's economy centers on agriculture (mainly wheat) and cattle; the Livestock Sales Pavilion still conducts a brisk business. Since 1966 the Plains Indians and Pioneers Museum has been open to visitors. Just north of town is Boiling Springs State Park with its natural springs which have supplied water to the town. The wooded area provides a lovely natural habitat for animals, and many years ago it was a favorite place of the Cheyenne and the Arapaho Indians.

Seldom has an individual been more closely identified with a home state than Will Rogers to Oklahoma. Born closer to Oolagah than Claremore, Rogers called Claremore his birthplace because, as he put it, "only an Indian can pronounce Oolagah."

He never tired of talking about his three-eighths Indian blood and Oklahoma ancestry. His ability to identify himself with the common man and small-town America endeared him to all who read his columns, saw his movies, or listened to him on the radio. Will Rogers never took himself or anyone else too seriously, and he worked harder than any two men, driving himself relentlessly. He questioned everything, but never lost his good-hearted nature.

In Will Rogers, people saw a man with a ready wit and uncommon common sense—a man who could complain without getting discouraged, who could find something positive to say about human nature and the human condition. He made his audiences shrug their shoulders and grin right along with him.

Even though Oklahoma lays claim to Will Rogers as a native son, Oklahomans are willing to share him with the folks in the rest of the country—and the world—who also made warm places in their hearts for him. This bust is in the state of Indiana.

The Will Rogers Memorial Museum and Tomb was dedicated on November 4, 1938, and was built of native stone quarried from Catoosa, only minutes away from the memorial.

The 20-acre site was purchased by Will Rogers himself for a retirement location. After his untimely death, his widow gave the property to the state, and the state built the museum. Each year many people visit to pay homage to a remarkable man.

This photograph, the only non-postcard in this book, was loaned by Mulhall historian Kathryn Stansbury. Although Rogers had already performed in front of an audience before working briefly with the Mulhall and 101 Wild West shows, these stints gave the humorist an excellent opportunity to exercise his enduring passion for roping.

The lady Will has circled with his lariat in this picture is Lucille Mulhall, the most talented cowgirl of all.

The term "cowgirl" was invented to describe Lucille Mulhall. She could rope, she could ride, and wrestle a steer to the ground—and she could do these things better than most men, a fact she proved in one rodeo contest after another.

Born in 1885, she began her show career as a young girl in her father's "Zack Mulhall's Wild West Show" and later, with the "101 Wild West Show." It was she, not Annie Oakley (an entertainer, rather than a real Western performer), who was regarded with enduring respect as the outstanding cowgirl.

Lucille Mulhall competed in what had been a man's world and she excelled in it. One statistic may prove the point: she could rope up to eight running horses at the same time.

As the successful Wild West shows proved, all the world loved the American West—or the dime-novelists' version of it.

The first and possibly the greatest show was created in the 1880's by William F. "Buffalo Bill" Cody. Although Cody had done scouting for the government, buffalo hunting, Pony Express riding, cowpunching, and even a bit of Indian fighting, his reputation as a cowboy was embellished by writers and his own promotion.

The story of his latter years is a sad one, ending in ill health and poverty, but before his death, Bill rode the show circuit with Pawnee Bill (whose real name was Gordon William Lillie) who had been a hunter, trapper, interpreter for the Pawnee Indians, and a rancher. He was even a leader of the Boomers into Oklahoma in April, 1889, having been hired by the Wichita, Kansas Board of Trade. After hearing of Cody's success and subsequent failure as a businessman, Lillie persuaded Buffalo Bill to join him in the Pawnee Bill Wild West Show which toured from 1908 to 1913.

While Buffalo Bill found it necessary to fulfill economic and contractual agreements by continually returning from retirement, Lillie turned his energies towards a variety of pursuits once his Wild West days were over. He became the author or co-author of five books dealing with Oklahoma history, the Pawnee Indians, his life with them, and Western lore. He also loaned his name and his time to a number of causes, including the Boy Scouts of America and an organization to preserve the buffalo. In addition, Lillie was director of Oklahoma's Historical Society, vice president of the Fern Oil Company, national supervisor of the Mounted Troops of America, President of the U.S. Highway 64 Association, and grand master of many celebrations. This picture showing Pawnee Bill with Lucille Mulhall was taken when he was 75 years old.

Lillie poses on horseback with Indians who performed in the "101 Wild West Show". This postcard is obviously from an earlier date than the card showing Lillie and Lucille Mulhall.

Bill's Indian Agency Trading Post, situated along Highway 64, is another example of Lillie's astute business sense—capitalizing on the tourist's fascination with the Indian and his own background as Pawnee interpreter and showman.

The story of how the "101 Wild West Show" began is worth telling. The most prominent character in the cast was patriarch Colonel George Miller, who died before the show became a money-making, touring troupe.

In 1871, Miller left his home in Crab Orchard, Kentucky, accompanied by his wife, Molly, and the first of their three boys, Joe, aged two. The Colonel settled first in Missouri where he deposited his family while he worked driving cattle from Texas to Kansas. Miller then moved to Kansas and later to Oklahoma where he built his enormous ranch near present-day Ponca City in the old Cherokee Outlet.

The Ponca Indians, led by Chief White Eagle who was a friend of the Colonel's, leased to him the 110,000 acres which became the ranch, Wild West Show headquarters, and base of operations for his various activities. According to Miller the "101" name resulted from a brawl involving his crew in a San Antonio saloon—the "101." Thereafter, he had his men use the 101 brand as a reminder. During the Colonel's lifetime, the ranch was very prosperous, so the decision to stage a local rodeo and cowboy show had little to do with making money. In 1904, after the Colonel's death, the troupe was invited to perform at the World's Fair in St. Louis.

CHIEF WHITE HORSE OF THE PONCA INDIANS AND LITTLE SOLDIER, 101 RANCH, OKLAHOMA.

At the time of the Colonel's death in 1903, the ranch was on a solid economic footing. Either already built or soon to be built were a tannery, blacksmith shop, creamery, jail, cafe, store, bunk houses, and other projects. When gas and oil were found on the ranch after 1910, the Miller boys built their own refinery. The sons—Joe, Zach, and George Lee—were largely responsible for this diversification, but the shrewdness and ingenuity inherited from the Colonel were their greatest assets.

Chief White Horse, pictured here, was befriended by the Colonel; he was a familiar fixture on the ranch and later in the 101 Wild West Shows.

Zachary Taylor Miller was the second son of Colonel Miller and, as this photo suggests, an excellent rider.

Zack was born in 1878 in Baxter Springs, Kansas. He was the last of the brothers to die, having lived long enough to see everything except the family residence put up for public auction. Unable in the end to finance or raise the money for another Wild West show comeback in the 1930's, Zack moved to Texas where he died in 1952.

COL. ZACK MILLER. (DOUBLECR.)

J. C. Miller and his Arabian Stallion "Ben Hur"
101 Ranch Real Wild West Show.

Joseph Carson Miller, eldest of Colonel Miller's sons, was generally known by his initials. J. C. may have been the most flamboyant of the boys. His show horse Pedro sported a $10,000 diamond-studded saddle.

About a year before their mother's death, George and Zack had a disagreement with Joe and bought out his share of the ranch. On her deathbed, Molly brought about a reconciliation of the brothers.

J. C. died in 1927 of carbon monoxide poisoning in his own garage; the death was deemed accidental.

In 1909 the second of the Miller's 101 Ranch residences burned down, and this big home called "The White House," was built. Indian rugs were scattered over the floors, show-piece rifles rested on pegs over the mantels, and Lenders' buffalo pictures were hung on the walls. The Ionic columns in front are an interesting embellishment to this frontier home. Although the house is large, it is hardly in the category of the homes that Oklahoma's oil barons were designing for themselves.

The "101 Wild West Show" had everything: rodeos, buffalo chases, fancy roping, fake gunfights, Indian exhibitions, and even a terrapin derby. The 1906 travelling troupe gives an idea of the show's size. Fifty Pullman and 100 freight cars were used for hauling the equipment, horses, and personnel.

After the "101 Wild West Show" took its first tour in 1906, the Miller brothers became more and more involved with it. This may have been a factor in the decline of the ranch's other activities and, eventually, of the ranch itself. Cattle, crops, and other ranch industries started to lose money as most of the boys' money, effort, and creativity were directed towards the show. Its road business progressed so well that the Millers took a European tour and appeared before the crowned heads of Europe.

The ranch itself became the training ground for the show, and for other rodeo and show business performers. Will Rogers loved to visit and would spend hours on the ranch practicing his lariat tricks.

TOM MIX, CHIEF OF COWBOYS, HAND-COLORED 101 RANCH, BLISS, OKLAHOMA,

One of the more irrepressible and richest early Western movie stars was Tom Mix. A native of Pennsylvania, Mix's early years were spent with his teamster father from whom he learned how to handle horses. After a brief period of military service, Mix wound up in Oklahoma where his fortunes underwent a change for the better.

Within a few years, Mix graduated from tending bar and riding with the "101 Wild West Show" to being a Deputy Marshal in Dewey, Oklahoma. A job with the Selig Polyscope Company as a livestock handler led him to California where he soon established himself as the celluloid cowboy, his best-known role. Always a man of action and extravagance, Mix went through a succession of wives who depleted his fortune even more quickly than he did with his propensity for nice homes, one of which had a beautiful Sohmer Welte (Licensee) reproducing grand piano; fine clothes; and fancy, fast automobiles. He died in 1940 when driving one of those fast cars, a late model Cord, he failed to negotiate a short detour involving some bridge construction and careened into an abutment near Florence, Arizona.

Mix never tired of embellishing his life story with fictional exploits that served as a tonic to millions of moviegoers who wanted larger-than-life heros.

The Osages were among the more colorful tribes in their native dress, although many tribes of the American Plains were known for headdresses, intricate beadwork, and leather stripping.

The Osage Indian seen here does not represent the tribe's typical daily dress; this sort of finery was reserved for the old and/or the influential, and was worn only on special occasions.

An Indian's manner of dress was usually determined by three factors: climate, cultural identity, and tribal status. Thus, the Apaches of Oklahoma wore one style of clothing when they were in the present-day Sooner State, and another (in this case, less clothing) when the Comanches displaced them to New Mexico and Arizona.

ONC-88—Osage Indian in Full Dress, Oklahoma

1A1051 **N**

The Osages, who inhabited Oklahoma since at least the seventeenth century, were a branch of what became known as the South Sioux Indians. They occupied land along the Arkansas River and its tributaries, but moved to the western part of the territory as the Five Civilized Tribes were driven into the eastern part of the future state in the 1820's.

The Osages were forced even further to the west by white settlements and the placement of various tribes in Oklahoma following the Civil War.

The Osages were buffalo hunters and farmers for several centuries before the discovery of oil on their land; the wealth that came with it was overwhelming. Unfortunately true are stories of Indians who bought new cars, then drove them until they ran out of gasoline or had a flat tire, then deserted the vehicle and simply purchased another. The white man's version of wealth often had little meaning for many of these people, for whom the finer things in life related more to clear blue sky, good hunting and fine harvests, tribal loyalties and love of the land.

The Comanches came to western Oklahoma from Wyoming at the beginning of the eighteenth century and served as a buffer to keep the Spanish in Texas and the northern Indians in Kansas. Within the tribe, the Comanche was friendly, even jovial; but centuries of self-reliance, war, and forced moves by the U.S. Government made them hostile to outsiders.

The Comanches were among Oklahoma's fiercest warriors, known for their harsh dealings with Kansas and Texas settlers homesteading on land they considered theirs and also for their defeat of the fierce Apaches. Cattle drives along the Chisholm and other Western trails, and wagon trains that traversed Comanche territory were frequently ambushed, with trail drivers being forced to give up all property in exchange for their lives.

COMANCHE INDIANS OF OKLAHOMA—17

Oklahoma has been the home of many talented Indian artists. One was Jerome Tiger, an exceptionally gifted Muskogee artist who died as a result of an accident while in his twenties.

Another was Acee Blue Eagle who lived a full, productive life which included military service in World War II. He was also honored to exhibit his art—and his dancing skill—at England's Oxford University. Blue Eagle was a Creek-Pawnee-Wichita Indian who lived in Muskogee and Okmulgee. He is best known for his ceremonial scenes and paintings of buffalo, wild horses, and antelope. Before his death and burial at the Fort Gibson Military Cemetery, Blue Eagle was listed in the International Who's Who and Who's Who of American Artists. He was also inducted into the Indian Hall of Fame.

Acee Blue Eagle, Famous Oklahoma Indian Artist

Muskogee and Okmulgee, Okla.   2C-H1092

ONS-393—Oklahoma Indian Girl

Identified only as "Oklahoma Indian Girl," this young lady models what appears to be a two-piece fringed outfit. By holding her elbows out she shows the piece to better advantage.

98

For the author, this postcard recalls scenes from his youth. Poor blacks, Indians, and Mexicans worked alongside equally indigent whites, filling bag after bag with the white crop.

Most fields of cotton were gathered at least three times. The first cotton was removed from the boll in which it grows. Until the fingers became toughened, the pricks of the pointed bolls were more than inconvenient; each morning for at least the first week of cotton picking pains like arthritis resulting from the jabs of these spears afflicted young and old alike.

The last gathering is referred to as "pulling

Picking Oklahoma Cotton.

bolls." By mid- to late August, the leaves of the cotton plant have dried, and the bolls themselves become brown and brittle. When the moisture content is thus reduced to almost nothing, bolls, leaves, and cotton were all gathered together. Bags of various lengths from six feet for the younger children to twelve feet for some of the more ambitious adults were filled again and again. Each bagful was weighed, immediate payment was given, and the worker with an empty container attacked another row.

During the 1940's and 1950's, the rate of pay was relatively constant: three cents for a pound of cotton and one and one-half cents for pulled bolls. One memory that will always remain vivid is the sound of spirituals sung by blacks in harmony or solo, their backs bent and their fingers flying among the plants.

Mistletoe is a parasite that attacks trees; nevertheless it has become a standard Christmas decoration.

There's a state that's rather new in the West;
Growing cotton, fruit, grain and all the rest,
So to you we'll make our bow—
Do it here and do it now—
Oklahoma and her products
are the best.

THE MISTLETOE
OKLAHOMA STATE FLOWER

6028

Mistletoe is the state flower of Oklahoma, and therein lies a tale. In Pottawatomie County in the winter of 1891, a young wife died of pneumonia, and her husband could find only some mistletoe to brighten the plain lumber of her homemade coffin. A neighbor, touched by the scene, promised to make mistletoe the state flower of Oklahoma if Oklahoma ever became a state. As a member of the Constitutional Convention some years later, the neighbor was able to keep his word.

The re-telling of the legend by Oklahomans suggests that although they are a tough and sturdy bunch, at heart they are romantics.

99

Will Rogers was a humorist rather than a comedian. A humorist attempts to use his skill to make his listeners think.

It has been maintained that no one in the past hundred years made his fellow human beings do more thinking, or more laughing, than did Will Rogers.

The most famous of Oklahoma's early photographers was William Prettyman. This postcard is derived from Prettyman's best-known picture, a real classic in the history of the state. For many years it was assumed that this was a picture of the 1889 Land Run but investigation proved it to be based on the photograph of the 1893 Cherokee Outlet Opening, taken at high noon, Sept. 16, 1893.

In the original photograph at the lower left is seen the back end of a wagon and the hats, shoulders, and and backs of seven men standing at the starting line, watching the mad rush.

WILL ROGERS

1889 Opening of Oklahoma "The Run"

ONC-64—Aerial View of the Approach to Grand River Dam, Northeastern Oklahoma

OC-H663

This postcard of the Grand River Dam, cancelled June 27, 1951, carries this description on the back:

Measuring 5680 feet, this is the longest multiple arch dam in the world. Its hydro-electric power plant has a capacity of 200,000,000 kilowatt hours. The beautiful lake, with an area of almost 50,000 acres, with more than a thousand miles of shore line makes this a perfect spot for fishing and boating.

The mailer of this card made his own notation—"The wind sure blows in Oklahoma."

Bacone College's Singing Redmen was a choral group composed of Indians from across the United States. In fact fourteen states and forty-two different tribes were represented at Muskogee's Bacone College. Its graduates served in education, Indian service and civil service positions; some continued their studies in areas such as law, medicine, and theology.

Alexander Posey, the Creek Indian poet, and Patrick J. Hurley, who served as Secretary of War during the administration of President Herbert Hoover and in various high-level diplomatic posts under President Franklin D. Roosevelt, were students at Bacone.

After a Hard Day's Ride

This postcard, cancelled at Bartlesville in 1909, shows the popular image of the cowboy and cowgirl. The style of dress shown here would be more appropriate at a rodeo or wild west show than "home on the range" where the real work took place.

THE SWEETHEART OF OKLAHOMA'S WHEAT COUNTRY

Wheat, cotton, oil and cattle are Oklahoma's products. Wheat's importance to the economy of Oklahoma, especially prior to World War II, was well-nigh inestimable. The back of this card carries the message from the writer: "I did not meet this young lady. I guess she was gone the day I came through the wheat field."

The Indian and the oil well, the "Sooner" nickname, and the state map are chosen to represent Oklahoma on this general Oklahoma postcard.

It's quite a state. It's quite a history.

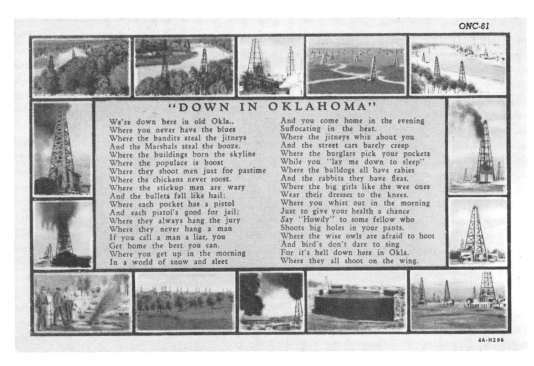

The poem reads in part:

We're down in Oklahoma/Where you never have the blues
Where the bandits steal the jitneys/and the marshals steal the booze.

Where you get up in the morning/in a world of snow and sleet/
and you come home in the evening suffocating in the heat.

Every place has its plusses and minuses; Oklahoma's no exception. But to those who love the state, there's just no place like home!

BIBLIOGRAPHY

Brown, Thomas Elton. *Bible Belt Catholicism: A History of the Roman Catholic Church in Oklahoma, 1905-1945.* Monograph Series 33. New York: United States Catholic Historical Society, 1977.

Collings, Ellsworth and Alma England. *The 101 Ranch.* Norman, Oklahoma: University of Oklahoma Press, 1937.

Cunningham, Robert E. *Stillwater: Where Oklahoma Began.* Stillwater, Oklahoma: Arts and Humanities Council of Stillwater, Oklahoma, Inc., 1969.

Dale, Edward Everett and Morris L. Wardell. *History of Oklahoma.* Englewood Cliffs, N. J.: Prentice)Hall, Inc., 1957.

Federal Writer's Program. *Oklahoma: A Guide to the Sooner State.* Norman, Oklahoma: University of Oklahoma, 1941.

Foreman, Grant. *A History of Oklahoma.* Norman, Oklahoma: University of Oklahoma Press, 1942.

Indian Territory: A Frontier Photographic Record by W. S. Prettyman. Edited by Robert E. Cunningham. Norman: University of Oklahoma Press, 1958.

Jayne, Velma Troxel and Stella Campbell Rockwell. *O County Faces and Places: A Collection of Cherokee Strip Photographs and Stories.* Enid, Oklahoma: Harold Allen, Printer. 1968.

Marriot, Alice and Carol Rachlin. *Oklahoma, the Forty-sixth Star,* Garden City, New York: Doubleday & Company, 1973.

McReynolds, Edwin C. *Oklahoma, a History of the Sooner State.* 4th ed. Norman, Oklahoma: University of Oklahoma Press, 1964.

McReynolds, Edwin C., et al. *Oklahoma, the Story of Its Past and Present.* Norman, Oklahoma: University of Oklahoma Press, 1985.

Oklahoma Historical Society. The Chronicles of Oklahoma. Vol. 31, No. 1. Oklahoma City, 1953.

Redway, J. W. and Russell Hinman. *Natural Complete Geography.* New York: American Book Company, 1912.

Shirk, George H. *Oklahoma Place Names.* 2nd Ed. Norman: University of Oklahoma Press, 1974.

Steinwehr, A. and D. G. Brinton. *Intermediate Geography.* Cincinnati: American Book Company, 1891.

Time-Life Books. *The End of the Myth.* Alexandria, Virginia, 1975.

_____. *The Great Chiefs.* Alexandria, Virginia, 1975.

_____. *The Gunfighters.* Alexandria, Virginia, 1975.

_____. *The Ranchers.* Alexandria, Virginia, 1975.

_____. *The Townsmen.* Alexandria, Virginia, 1975.

INDEX